EVERYMAN'S LIBRARY
POCKET POETS

TENNYSON

POEMS

EVERYMAN'S LIBRARY
POCKET POETS

Alfred A. Knopf New York London Toronto

THIS IS A BORZOI BOOK

PUBLISHED BY ALFRED A. KNOPF

This selection by Peter Washington first published in
Everyman's Library, 2004
Copyright © 2004 by Everyman's Library
Eighth printing (US)

All rights reserved. Published in the United States by Alfred A. Knopf, a division of Penguin Random House LLC, New York, and in Canada by Penguin Random House Canada Limited, Toronto. Distributed by Penguin Random House LLC, New York. Published in the United Kingdom by Everyman's Library, 50 Albemarle Street, London W1S 4BD and distributed by Penguin Random House UK, 20 Vauxhall Bridge Road, London SW1V 2SA.

www.randomhouse.com/everymans
www.everymanslibrary.co.uk

ISBN 978-1-4000-4187-9 (US)
978-1-84159-759-1 (UK)

A CIP catalogue record for this book is available from the British Library

Library of Congress Cataloging-in-Publication Data
Tennyson, Alfred Tennyson, Baron, 1809–1892.
[Poems. Selections]
Poems / Tennyson.
p. cm.—(Everyman's library pocket poets)
ISBN 978-1-4000-4187-9 (hc : alk. paper)
I. Title: Tennyson. II. Title. III. Series.
PR5551 2004
821'.8—dc22 2003049505

Typography by Peter B. Willberg

Typeset in the UK by AccComputing, North Barrow, Somerset

Printed and bound in Germany by GGP Media GmbH, Pössneck

CONTENTS

NARRATIVE POEMS

ABOUT POETRY

PUBLIC VERSE

FRAGMENTS AND EXPERIMENTS

EPIGRAMS

ALFRED, LORD TENNYSON

POEMS

JUNE BRACKEN AND HEATHER

to Emily Tennyson

There on the top of the down,
The wild heather round me and over me June's
    high blue,
When I looked at the bracken so bright and the heather
    so brown,
I thought to myself I would offer this book to you,
This, and my love together,
To you that are seventy-seven,
With a faith as clear as the heights of the June-blue
    heaven,
And a fancy as summer-new
As the green of the bracken amid the gloom
    of the heather.

SONGS LYRIC AND DRAMATIC

LOVE'S LATEST HOUR IS THIS

Love's latest hour is this,
True love from love must part,
Yet ere I lose my bliss,
Sweet! let me feel thine heart.
One Kiss! one Kiss! One Kiss!
Cling, clasp me heart to heart!

One Kiss! I scarce can speak,
And thy lips tremble now.
Yet let me kiss thy cheek,
Ah! let me kiss thy brow!
One on thy neck, thy cheek,
Another on thy brow!

I go: the day steals on.
Henceforth I hate the skies.
I go: my hope is gone.
Yet let me kiss thine eyes!
I go: not yet! yet one,
One Kiss between thine eyes!

How sweet to stand embraced
Till I grow stiff and cold
In folding thy dear waist
Which I no more shall fold;

Dear lips! Dear eyes! Dear waist!
Which I no more shall fold.

The world is nothing worth,
Here let me fall and lie;
What is there else on earth?
'Twere better far to die!
Lay lip to lip! Pluck forth
My heart that I may die!

TO A LADY SLEEPING

O thou whose fringèd lids I gaze upon,
Through whose dim brain the wingèd dreams
are borne,
Unroof the shrines of clearest vision,
In honour of the silverfleckèd morn:
Long hath the white wave of the virgin light
Driven back the billow of the dreamful dark.
Thou all unwittingly prolongest night,
Though long ago listening the poisèd lark,
With eyes dropt downward through the blue serene,
Over heaven's parapets the angels lean.

WHISPERS

'Tis not alone the warbling woods,
The starred abysses of the sky,
The silent hills, the stormy floods,
The green that fills the eye –
These only do not move the breast;
Like some wise artist, Nature gives,
Through all her works, to each that lives
A hint of somewhat unexprest.

Whate'er I see, where'er I move,
These whispers rise, and fall away,
Something of pain – of bliss – of Love,
But what, were hard to say.
I could not tell it: if I could
Yet every form of mind is made
To vary in some light or shade
So were my tale misunderstood.

KATE

I know her by her angry air,
Her brightblack eyes, her brightblack hair,
    Her rapid laughters wild and shrill,
As laughter of the woodpecker
    From the bosom of a hill.
    'Tis Kate – she sayeth what she will:
For Kate hath an unbridled tongue,
    Clear as the twanging of a harp.
        Her heart is like a throbbing star.
Kate hath a spirit ever strung
    Like a new bow, and bright and sharp
        As edges of the scymetar.
Whence shall she take a fitting mate?
    For Kate no common love will feel;
My woman-soldier, gallant Kate,
    As pure and true as blades of steel.

Kate saith 'the world is void of might.'
    Kate saith 'the men are gilded flies.'
        Kate snaps her fingers at my vows;
    Kate will not hear of lover's sighs.
I would I were an armèd knight,
    Far-famed for well-won enterprise,
        And wearing on my swarthy brows
    The garland of new-wreathed emprise;

For in a moment I would pierce
The blackest files of clanging fight,
And strongly strike to left and right,
In dreaming of my lady's eyes.
Oh! Kate loves well the bold and fierce;
But none are bold enough for Kate,
She cannot find a fitting mate.

MARIANA

'Mariana in the moated grange'
– *Measure for Measure*

With blackest moss the flower-plots
Were thickly crusted, one and all:
The rusted nails fell from the knots
That held the pear to the garden-wall.
The broken sheds looked sad and strange:
Unlifted was the clinking latch;
Weeded and worn the ancient thatch
Upon the lonely moated grange.
She only said, 'My life is dreary,
He cometh not,' she said;
She said, 'I am aweary, aweary,
I would that I were dead!'

Her tears fell with the dews at even;
  Her tears fell ere the dews were dried;
She could not look on the sweet heaven,
  Either at morn or eventide.
After the flitting of the bats,
  When thickest dark did trance the sky,
  She drew her casement-curtain by,
And glanced athwart the glooming flats.
    She only said, 'The night is dreary,
      He cometh not,' she said;
    She said, 'I am aweary, aweary,
      I would that I were dead!'

Upon the middle of the night,
  Waking she heard the night-fowl crow:
The cock sung out an hour ere light:
  From the dark fen the oxen's low
Came to her: without hope of change,
  In sleep she seemed to walk forlorn,
  Till cold winds woke the grey-eyed morn
About the lonely moated grange.
    She only said, 'The day is dreary,
      He cometh not,' she said;
    She said, 'I am aweary, aweary,
      I would that I were dead!'

About a stone-cast from the wall
  A sluice with blackened waters slept,
And o'er it many, round and small,
  The clustered marish-mosses crept.
Hard by a poplar shook alway,
  All silver-green with gnarlèd bark:
  For leagues no other tree did mark
The level waste, the rounding grey.
    She only said, 'My life is dreary,
      He cometh not,' she said;
    She said, 'I am aweary, aweary,
      I would that I were dead!'

And ever when the moon was low,
  And the shrill winds were up and away,
In the white curtain, to and fro,
  She saw the gusty shadow sway.
But when the moon was very low,
  And wild winds bound within their cell,
  The shadow of the poplar fell
Upon her bed, across her brow.
    She only said, 'The night is dreary,
      He cometh not,' she said;
    She said, 'I am aweary, aweary,
      I would that I were dead!'

All day within the dreamy house,
The doors upon their hinges creaked;
The blue fly sung in the pane; the mouse
Behind the mouldering wainscot shrieked,
Or from the crevice peered about.
Old faces glimmered through the doors,
Old footsteps trod the upper floors,
Old voices called her from without.
She only said, 'My life is dreary,
He cometh not,' she said;
She said, 'I am aweary, aweary,
I would that I were dead!'

The sparrow's chirrup on the roof,
The slow clock ticking, and the sound
Which to the wooing wind aloof
The poplar made, did all confound
Her sense; but most she loathed the hour
When the thick-moted sunbeam lay
Athwart the chambers, and the day
Was sloping toward his western bower.
Then, said she, 'I am very dreary,
He will not come,' she said;
She wept, 'I am aweary, aweary,
Oh God, that I were dead!'

THREE SONNETS TO A COQUETTE

I

Caressed or chidden by the dainty hand,
  And singing airy trifles this or that,
Light Hope at Beauty's call would perch and stand,
  And run through every change of sharp and flat;
  And Fancy came and at her pillow sat,
When Sleep had bound her in his rosy band,
  And chased away the still-recurring gnat,
And woke her with a lay from fairy land.
But now they live with Beauty less and less,
  For Hope is other Hope and wanders far,
    Nor cares to lisp in love's delicious creeds;
And Fancy watches in the wilderness,
  Poor Fancy sadder than a single star,
    That sets at twilight in a land of reeds.

II

The form, the form alone is eloquent!
  A nobler yearning never broke her rest
  Than but to dance and sing, be gaily drest,
And win all eyes with all accomplishment:
Yet in the waltzing-circle as we went,
  My fancy made me for a moment blest
  To find my heart so near the beauteous breast
That once had power to rob it of content.

A moment came the tenderness of tears,
  The phantom of a wish, that once could move,
    A ghost of passion that no smiles restore –
  For ah! the slight coquette, she cannot love,
And if you kissed her feet a thousand years,
  She still would take the praise, and care no more.

III

Wan Sculptor, weepest thou to take the cast
  Of those dead lineaments that near thee lie?
Or sorrowest thou, pale Painter, for the past,
  In painting some dead friend from memory?
Weep on: beyond his object Love can last:
  His object lives: more cause to weep have I:
My tears, no tears of love, are flowing fast,
  No tears of love, but tears that Love can die.
I pledge her not in any cheerful cup,
  Nor care to sit beside her where she sits –
    Ah pity – hint it not in human tones,
But breathe it into earth and close it up
  With secret death for ever, in the pits
    Which some green Christmas crams with
      weary bones.

SONNET

As when with downcast eyes we muse and brood,
And ebb into a former life, or seem
To lapse far back in some confusèd dream
To states of mystical similitude;
If one but speaks or hems or stirs his chair,
Ever the wonder waxeth more and more,
So that we say, 'All this hath been before,
All this *hath* been, I know not when or where.'
So, friend, when first I looked upon your face,
Our thought gave answer, each to each, so true,
Opposèd mirrors each reflecting each –
That though I knew not in what time or place,
Methought that I had often met with you,
And each had lived in either's heart and speech.

ST AGNES' EVE

Deep on the convent-roof the snows
  Are sparkling to the moon:
My breath to heaven like vapour goes:
  May my soul follow soon!
The shadows of the convent-towers
  Slant down the snowy sward,
Still creeping with the creeping hours
  That lead me to my Lord:
Make Thou my spirit pure and clear
  As are the frosty skies,
Or this first snowdrop of the year
  That in my bosom lies.

As these white robes are soiled and dark,
  To yonder shining ground;
As this pale taper's earthly spark,
  To yonder argent round;
So shows my soul before the Lamb,
  My spirit before Thee;
So in mine earthly house I am,
  To that I hope to be.
Break up the heavens, O Lord! and far,
  Through all yon starlight keen,
Draw me, thy bride, a glittering star,
  In raiment white and clean.

He lifts me to the golden doors;
    The flashes come and go;
All heaven bursts her starry floors,
    And strows her lights below,
And deepens on and up! the gates
    Roll back, and far within
For me the Heavenly Bridegroom waits,
    To make me pure of sin.
The sabbaths of Eternity,
    One sabbath deep and wide –
A light upon the shining sea –
    The Bridegroom with his bride!

FLOWER IN THE CRANNIED WALL

Flower in the crannied wall,
I pluck you out of the crannies,
I hold you here, root and all, in my hand,
Little flower – but *if* I could understand
What you are, root and all, and all in all,
I should know what God and man is.

LEONINE ELEGIACS

Low-flowing breezes are roaming the broad valley
dimmed in the gloaming:
Through the black-stemmed pines only the far river shines.
Creeping through blossomy rushes and bowers of
rose-blowing bushes,
Down by the poplar tall rivulets babble and fall.
Barketh the shepherd-dog cheerly; the grasshopper
carolleth clearly;
Deeply the wood-dove coos; shrilly the owlet halloos;
Winds creep; dews fall chilly: in her first sleep earth
breathes stilly:
Over the pools in the burn water-gnats murmur
and mourn.
Sadly the far kine loweth: the glimmering water
outfloweth:
Twin peaks shadowed with pine slope to the dark hyaline.
Low-throned Hesper is stayèd between the two peaks;
but the Naiad
Throbbing in mild unrest holds him beneath in her breast.
The ancient poetess singeth, that Hesperus all things
bringeth,
Smoothing the wearied mind: bring me my love, Rosalind.
Thou comest morning and even; she cometh not morning
or even.
False-eyed Hesper, unkind, where is my sweet Rosalind?

BREAK, BREAK, BREAK

Break, break, break,
  On thy cold grey stones, O Sea!
And I would that my tongue could utter
  The thoughts that arise in me.

O well for the fisherman's boy,
  That he shouts with his sister at play!
O well for the sailor lad,
  That he sings in his boat on the bay!

And the stately ships go on
  To their haven under the hill;
But O for the touch of a vanished hand,
  And the sound of a voice that is still!

Break, break, break,
  At the foot of thy crags, O Sea!
But the tender grace of a day that is dead
  Will never come back to me.

IN THE VALLEY OF CAUTERETZ

All along the valley, stream that flashest white,
Deepening thy voice with the deepening of the night,
All along the valley, where thy waters flow,
I walked with one I loved two and thirty years ago.
All along the valley while I walked to-day,
The two and thirty years were a mist that rolls away;
For all along the valley, down thy rocky bed
Thy living voice to me was as the voice of the dead,
And all along the valley, by rock and cave and tree,
The voice of the dead was a living voice to me.

LOVE AND DEATH

What time the mighty moon was gathering light
Love paced the thymy plots of Paradise,
And all about him rolled his lustrous eyes;
When, turning round a cassia, full in view
Death, walking all alone beneath a yew,
And talking to himself, first met his sight:
'You must begone,' said Death, 'these walks are mine.'
Love wept and spread his sheeny vans for flight;
Yet ere he parted said, 'This hour is thine:
Thou art the shadow of life, and as the tree

Stands in the sun and shadows all beneath,
So in the light of great eternity
Life eminent creates the shade of death;
The shadow passeth when the tree shall fall,
But I shall reign for ever over all.'

SONG

A spirit haunts the year's last hours
Dwelling amid these yellowing bowers:
        To himself he talks;
For at eventide, listening earnestly,
At his work you may hear him sob and sigh
        In the walks;
        Earthward he boweth the heavy stalks
Of the mouldering flowers:
        Heavily hangs the broad sunflower
            Over its grave i' the earth so chilly;
        Heavily hangs the hollyhock,
            Heavily hangs the tiger-lily.

The air is damp, and hushed, and close,
As a sick man's room when he taketh repose
        An hour before death;
My very heart faints and my whole soul grieves

At the moist rich smell of the rotting leaves,
And the breath
Of the fading edges of box beneath,
And the year's last rose.
Heavily hangs the broad sunflower
Over its grave i' the earth so chilly;
Heavily hangs the hollyhock,
Heavily hangs the tiger-lily.

From THE PRINCESS

I

As through the land at eve we went,
And plucked the ripened ears,
We fell out, my wife and I
O we fell out I know not why,
And kissed again with tears.
And blessings on the falling out
That all the more endears,
When we fall out with those we love
And kiss again with tears!
For when we came where lies the child
We lost in other years,
There above the little grave,
O there above the little grave,
We kissed again with tears.

II

Sweet and low, sweet and low,
  Wind of the western sea,
Low, low, breathe and blow,
  Wind of the western sea!
Over the rolling waters go
Come from the dying moon, and blow,
  Blow him again to me;
While my little one, while my pretty one, sleeps.

Sleep and rest, sleep and rest,
  Father will come to thee soon;
Rest, rest, on mother's breast,
  Father will come to thee soon;
Father will come to his babe in the nest,
Silver sails all out of the west
  Under the silver moon:
Sleep, my little one, sleep, my pretty one, sleep.

III

The splendour falls on castle walls
  And snowy summits old in story:
The long light shakes across the lakes,
  And the wild cataract leaps in glory.
Blow, bugle, blow, set the wild echoes flying,
Blow, bugle; answer, echoes, dying, dying, dying.

O hark, O hear! how thin and clear,
And thinner, clearer, farther going!
O sweet and far from cliff and scar
The horns of Elfland faintly blowing!
Blow, let us hear the purple glens replying:
Blow, bugle; answer, echoes, dying, dying, dying.

O love, they die in yon rich sky,
They faint on hill or field or river:
Our echoes roll from soul to soul,
And grow for ever and for ever.
Blow, bugle, blow, set the wild echoes flying,
And answer, echoes, dying, dying, dying.

IV

Tears, idle tears, I know not what they mean,
Tears from the depth of some divine despair
Rise in the heart, and gather to the eyes,
In looking on the happy Autumn-fields,
And thinking of the days that are no more.

Fresh as the first beam glittering on a sail,
That brings our friends up from the underworld,
Sad as the last which reddens over one
That sinks with all we love below the verge;
So sad, so fresh, the days that are no more.

Ah, sad and strange as in dark summer dawns
The earliest pipe of half-awakened birds
To dying ears, when unto dying eyes
The casement slowly grows a glimmering square;
So sad, so strange, the days that are no more.

Dear as remembered kisses after death,
And sweet as those by hopeless fancy feigned
On lips that are for others; deep as love,
Deep as first love, and wild with all regret;
O Death in Life, the days that are no more.

V

O Swallow, Swallow, flying, flying South,
Fly to her, and fall upon her gilded eaves,
And tell her, tell her, what I tell to thee.

O tell her, Swallow, thou that knowest each,
That bright and fierce and fickle is the South,
And dark and true and tender is the North.

O Swallow, Swallow, if I could follow, and light
Upon her lattice, I would pipe and trill,
And cheep and twitter twenty million loves.

O were I thou that she might take me in,
And lay me on her bosom, and her heart
Would rock the snowy cradle till I died.

Why lingereth she to clothe her heart with love,
Delaying as the tender ash delays
To clothe herself, when all the woods are green?

O tell her, Swallow, that thy brood is flown:
Say to her, I do but wanton in the South,
But in the North long since my nest is made.

O tell her, brief is life but love is long,
And brief the sun of summer in the North,
And brief the moon of beauty in the South.

O Swallow, flying from the golden woods,
Fly to her, and pipe and woo her, and make her mine,
And tell her, tell her, that I follow thee.

VI

Home they brought her warrior dead:
  She nor swooned, nor uttered cry:
All her maidens, watching, said,
  'She must weep or she will die.'

Then they praised him, soft and low,
  Called him worthy to be loved,
Truest friend and noblest foe;
  Yet she neither spoke nor moved.

Stole a maiden from her place,
Lightly to the warrior stept,
Took the face cloth from the face:
Yet she neither moved nor wept.

Rose a nurse of ninety years,
Set his child upon her knee –
Like summer tempest came her tears –
'Sweet my child, I live for thee.'

VII

Ask me no more: the moon may draw the sea;
The cloud may stoop from heaven and take the shape,
With fold to fold, of mountain or of cape;
But O too fond, when have I answered thee?
Ask me no more.

Ask me no more: what answer should I give?
I love not hollow cheek or faded eye:
Yet, O my friend, I will not have thee die!
Ask me no more, lest I should bid thee live;
Ask me no more.

Ask me no more: thy fate and mine are sealed:
I strove against the stream and all in vain:
Let the great river take me to the main:
No more, dear love, for at a touch I yield;
Ask me no more.

VIII

Now sleeps the crimson petal, now the white;
Nor waves the cypress in the palace walk;
Nor winks the gold fin in the porphyry font:
The fire-fly wakens: waken thou with me.

Now droops the milkwhite peacock like a ghost,
And like a ghost she glimmers on to me.

Now lies the earth all Danaë to the stars,
And all thy heart lies open unto me.

Now slides the silent meteor on, and leaves
A shining furrow, all thy thoughts in me.

Now folds the lily all her sweetness up,
And slips into the bosom of the lake:
So fold thyself, my dearest, thou, and slip
Into my bosom and be lost in me.

IX

Come down, O maid, from yonder mountain height:
What pleasure lives in height (the shepherd sang)
In height and cold, the splendour of the hills?
But cease to move so near the Heavens, and cease
To glide a sunbeam by the blasted Pine,
To sit a star upon the sparkling spire;

And come, for Love is of the valley, come,
For Love is of the valley, come thou down
And find him; by the happy threshold, he,
Or hand in hand with Plenty in the maize,
Or red with spirted purple of the vats,
Or foxlike in the vine; nor cares to walk
With Death and Morning on the silver horns,
Nor wilt thou snare him in the white ravine,
Nor find him dropt upon the firths of ice,
That huddling slant in furrow-cloven falls
To roll the torrent out of dusky doors:
But follow; let the torrent dance thee down
To find him in the valley; let the wild
Lean-headed Eagles yelp alone, and leave
The monstrous ledges there to slope, and spill
Their thousand wreaths of dangling water-smoke,
That like a broken purpose waste in air:
So waste not thou, but come, for all the vales
Await thee; azure pillars of the hearth
Arise to thee; the children call, and I
Thy shepherd pipe, and sweet is every sound,
Sweeter thy voice, but every sound is sweet;
Myriads of rivulets hurrying through the lawn,
The moan of doves in immemorial elms,
And murmuring of innumerable bees.

MOVE EASTWARD, HAPPY EARTH

Move eastward, happy earth, and leave
 Yon orange sunset waning slow:
From fringes of the faded eve,
 O, happy planet, eastward go;
Till over thy dark shoulder glow
 Thy silver sister-world, and rise
To glass herself in dewy eyes
 That watch me from the glen below.

Ah, bear me with thee, smoothly borne,
 Dip forward under starry light,
And move me to my marriage-morn,
 And round again to happy night.

From THE DAY-DREAM: THE REVIVAL

A touch, a kiss! the charm was snapt.
 There rose a noise of striking clocks,
And feet that ran, and doors that clapt,
 And barking dogs, and crowing cocks;
A fuller light illumined all,
 A breeze through all the garden swept,
A sudden hubbub shook the hall
 And sixty feet the fountain leapt.

The hedge broke in, the banner blew,
  The butler drank, the steward scrawled,
The fire shot up, the martin flew,
  The parrot screamed, the peacock squalled,
The maid and page renewed their strife,
  The palace banged, and buzzed and clackt,
And all the long-pent stream of life
  Dashed downward in a cataract.

And last with these the king awoke,
  And in his chair himself upreared,
And yawned, and rubbed his face, and spoke,
  'By holy rood, a royal beard!
How say you? we have slept, my lords.
  My beard has grown into my lap.'
The barons swore, with many words,
  'Twas but an after-dinner's nap.

'Pardy,' returned the king, 'but still
  My joints are something stiff or so.
My lord, and shall we pass the bill
  I mentioned half an hour ago?'
The chancellor, sedate and vain,
  In courteous words returned reply:
But dallied with his golden chain,
  And, smiling, put the question by.

THE KRAKEN

Below the thunders of the upper deep;
Far, far beneath in the abysmal sea,
His ancient, dreamless, uninvaded sleep
The Kraken sleepeth: faintest sunlights flee
About his shadowy sides: above him swell
Huge sponges of millennial growth and height;
And far away into the sickly light,
From many a wondrous grot and secret cell
Unnumbered and enormous polypi
Winnow with giant fins the slumbering green.
There hath he lain for ages and will lie
Battening upon huge seaworms in his sleep,
Until the latter fire shall heat the deep;
Then once by men and angels to be seen,
In roaring he shall rise and on the surface die.

THE OWL

When cats run home and light is come,
  And dew is cold upon the ground,
And the far-off stream is dumb,
  And the whirring sail goes round,
  And the whirring sail goes round;
    Alone and warming his five wits,
    The white owl in the belfry sits.

When merry milkmaids click the latch,
  And rarely smells the new-mown hay,
And the cock hath sung beneath the thatch
  Twice or thrice his roundelay,
  Twice or thrice his roundelay;
    Alone and warming his five wits,
    The white owl in the belfry sits.

THE EAGLE *(Fragment)*

He clasps the crag with crooked hands;
Close to the sun in lonely lands,
Ringed with the azure world, he stands.

The wrinkled sea beneath him crawls;
He watches from his mountain walls,
And like a thunderbolt he falls.

THE BLACKBIRD

O Blackbird! sing me something well:
  While all the neighbours shoot thee round,
  I keep smooth plats of fruitful ground,
Where thou may'st warble, eat and dwell.

The espaliers and the standards all
  Are thine; the range of lawn and park:
  The unnetted black-hearts ripen dark,
All thine, against the garden wall.

Yet, though I spared thee all the spring,
  Thy sole delight is, sitting still,
  With that gold dagger of thy bill
To fret the summer jenneting.

A golden bill! the silver tongue,
  Cold February loved, is dry:
  Plenty corrupts the melody
That made thee famous once, when young:

And in the sultry garden-squares,
  Now thy flute-notes are changed to coarse,
  I hear thee not at all, or hoarse
As when a hawker hawks his wares.

Take warning! he that will not sing
　While yon sun prospers in the blue,
　Shall sing for want, ere leaves are new,
Caught in the frozen palms of Spring.

THE DYING SWAN

The plain was grassy, wild and bare,
Wide, wild, and open to the air,
Which had built up everywhere
　An under-roof of doleful grey.
With an inner voice the river ran,
Adown it floated a dying swan,
　　And loudly did lament.
　It was the middle of the day.
Ever the weary wind went on,
　　And took the reed-tops as it went.

Some blue peaks in the distance rose,
And white against the cold-white sky,
Shone out their crowning snows.
　One willow over the river wept,
And shook the wave as the wind did sigh;
Above in the wind was the swallow,
　Chasing itself at its own wild will,

And far through the marish green and still
The tangled water-courses slept,
Shot over with purple, and green, and yellow.

The wild swan's death-hymn took the soul
Of that waste place with joy
Hidden in sorrow: at first to the ear
The warble was low, and full and clear;
And floating about the under-sky,
Prevailing in weakness, the coronach stole
Sometimes afar, and sometimes anear;
But anon her awful jubilant voice,
With a music strange and manifold,
Flowed forth on a carol free and bold;
As when a mighty people rejoice
With shawms, and with cymbals, and harps of gold,
And the tumult of their acclaim is rolled
Through the open gates of the city afar,
To the shepherd who watcheth the evening star.
And the creeping mosses and clambering weeds,
And the willow-branches hoar and dank,
And the wavy swell of the soughing reeds,
And the wave-worn horns of the echoing bank,
And the silvery marish-flowers that throng
The desolate creeks and pools among,
Were flooded over with eddying song.

From MAUD

I

O let the solid ground
  Not fail beneath my feet
Before my life has found
  What some have found so sweet;
Then let come what come may,
What matter if I go mad,
I shall have had my day.

Let the sweet heavens endure,
  Not close and darken above me
Before I am quite quite sure
  That there is one to love me;
Then let come what come may
To a life that has been so sad,
I shall have had my day.

II

Birds in the high Hall-garden
  When twilight was falling,
Maud, Maud, Maud, Maud,
  They were crying and calling.

Where was Maud? in our wood;
  And I, who else, was with her,

Gathering woodland lilies,
  Myriads blow together.

Birds in our wood sang
  Ringing through the valleys,
Maud is here, here, here
  In among the lilies.

I kissed her slender hand,
  She took the kiss sedately;
Maud is not seventeen,
  But she is tall and stately.

I to cry out on pride
  Who have won her favour!
O Maud were sure of Heaven
  If lowliness could save her.

I know the way she went
  Home with her maiden posy,
For her feet have touched the meadows
  And left the daisies rosy.

Birds in the high Hall-garden
  Were crying and calling to her,
Where is Maud, Maud, Maud?
  One is come to woo her.

Look, a horse at the door,
  And little King Charley snarling,
Go back, my lord, across the moor,
  You are not her darling.

III

Go not, happy day,
  From the shining fields,
Go not, happy day,
  Till the maiden yields.
Rosy is the West,
  Rosy is the South,
Roses are her cheeks,
  And a rose her mouth.
When the happy Yes
  Falters from her lips,
Pass and blush the news
  O'er the blowing ships.
Over blowing seas,
  Over seas at rest,
Pass the happy news,
  Blush it through the West;
Till the red man dance
  By his red cedar tree,
And the red man's babe
  Leap, beyond the sea.
Blush from West to East,

Blush from East to West,
Till the West is East,
Blush it through the West.
Rosy is the West,
Rosy is the South,
Roses are her cheeks
And a rose her mouth.

IV

Come into the garden, Maud,
For the black bat, night, has flown,
Come into the garden, Maud,
I am here at the gate alone;
And the woodbine spices are wafted abroad,
And the musk of the rose is blown.

For a breeze of morning moves,
And the planet of Love is on high,
Beginning to faint in the light that she loves
On a bed of daffodil sky,
To faint in the light of the sun she loves,
To faint in his light, and to die.

All night have the roses heard
The flute, violin, bassoon;
All night has the casement jessamine stirred
To the dancers dancing in tune;

Till a silence fell with the waking bird,
  And a hush with the setting moon.

I said to the lily, 'There is but one
  With whom she has heart to be gay.
When will the dancers leave her alone?
  She is weary of dance and play.'
Now half to the setting moon are gone,
  And half to the rising day;
Low on the sand and loud on the stone
  The last wheel echoes away.

I said to the rose, 'The brief night goes
  In babble and revel and wine.
O young lord-lover, what sighs are those,
  For one that will never be thine?
But mine, but mine,' so I sware to the rose,
  'For ever and ever, mine.'

And the soul of the rose went into my blood,
  As the music clashed in the hall;
And long by the garden lake I stood,
  For I heard your rivulet fall
From the lake to the meadow and on to the wood,
  Our wood, that is dearer than all;

From the meadow your walks have left so sweet
  That whenever a March-wind sighs
He sets the jewel-print of your feet
  In violets blue as your eyes,
To the woody hollows in which we meet
  And the valleys of Paradise.

The slender acacia would not shake
  One long milk-bloom on the tree;
The white lake-blossom fell into the lake
  As the pimpernel dozed on the lea;
But the rose was awake all night for your sake,
  Knowing your promise to me;
The lilies and roses were all awake,
  They sighed for the dawn and thee.

Queen rose of the rosebud garden of girls,
  Come hither, the dances are done,
In gloss of satin and glimmer of pearls,
  Queen lily and rose in one;
Shine out, little head, sunning over with curls,
  To the flowers, and be their sun.

There has fallen a splendid tear
  From the passion-flower at the gate.
She is coming, my dove, my dear;
  She is coming, my life, my fate;

The red rose cries, 'She is near, she is near;'
  And the white rose weeps, 'She is late;'
The larkspur listens, 'I hear, I hear;'
  And the lily whispers, 'I wait.'

She is coming, my own, my sweet;
  Were it ever so airy a tread,
My heart would hear her and beat,
  Were it earth in an earthy bed;
My dust would hear her and beat,
  Had I lain for a century dead;
Would start and tremble under her feet,
  And blossom in purple and red.

V

O that 'twere possible
After long grief and pain
To find the arms of my true love
Round me once again!

When I was wont to meet her
In the silent woody places
By the home that gave me birth,
We stood tranced in long embraces
Mixt with kisses sweeter sweeter
Than any thing on earth.

A shadow flits before me,
Not thou, but like to thee;
Ah Christ, that it were possible
For one short hour to see
The souls we loved, that they might tell us
What and where they be.

It leads me forth at evening,
It lightly winds and steals
In a cold white robe before me,
When all my spirit reels
At the shouts, the leagues of lights,
And the roaring of the wheels.

Half the night I waste in sighs,
Half in dreams I sorrow after
The delight of early skies;
In a wakeful doze I sorrow
For the hand, the lips, the eyes,
For the meeting of the morrow,
The delight of happy laughter,
The delight of low replies.

'Tis a morning pure and sweet,
And a dewy splendour falls
On the little flower that clings
To the turrets and the walls;

'Tis a morning pure and sweet,
And the light and shadow fleet;
She is walking in the meadow,
And the woodland echo rings;
In a moment we shall meet;
She is singing in the meadow,
And the rivulet at her feet
Ripples on in light and shadow
To the ballad that she sings.

Do I hear her sing as of old,
My bird with the shining head,
My own dove with the tender eye?
But there rings on a sudden a passionate cry,
There is some one dying or dead,
And a sullen thunder is rolled;
For a tumult shakes the city,
And I wake, my dream is fled;
In the shuddering dawn, behold,
Without knowledge, without pity,
By the curtains of my bed
That abiding phantom cold.

Get thee hence, nor come again,
Mix not memory with doubt
Pass, thou deathlike type of pain,
Pass and cease to move about!

'Tis the blot upon the brain
That *will* show itself without.

Then I rise, the eavedrops fall,
And the yellow vapours choke
The great city sounding wide;
The day comes, a dull red ball
Wrapt in drifts of lurid smoke
On the misty river-tide.

Through the hubbub of the market
I steal, a wasted frame,
It crosses here, it crosses there,
Through all that crowd confused and loud,
The shadow still the same;
And on my heavy eyelids
My anguish hangs like shame.

Alas for her that met me,
That heard me softly call,
Came glimmering through the laurels
At the quiet evenfall,
In the garden by the turrets
Of the old manorial hall.

Would the happy spirit descend,
From the realms of light and song,
In the chamber or the street,
As she looks among the blest,
Should I fear to greet my friend
Or to say 'forgive the wrong,'
Or to ask her, 'take me, sweet,
To the regions of thy rest'?

But the broad light glares and beats,
And the shadow flits and fleets
And will not let me be;
And I loathe the squares and streets,
And the faces that one meets,
Hearts with no love for me:
Always I long to creep
Into some still cavern deep,
There to weep, and weep, and weep
My whole soul out to thee.

TO EDWARD LEAR ON HIS TRAVELS IN GREECE

Illyrian woodlands, echoing falls
  Of water, sheets of summer glass,
  The long divine Peneïan pass,
The vast Akrokeraunian walls,

Tomohrit, Athos, all things fair,
  With such a pencil, such a pen,
  You shadow forth to distant men,
I read and felt that I was there:

And trust me while I turned the page,
  And tracked you still on classic ground,
  I grew in gladness till I found
My spirits in the golden age.

For me the torrent ever poured
  And glistened – here and there alone
  The broad-limbed Gods at random thrown
By fountain-urns; – and Naiads oared

A glimmering shoulder under gloom
  Of cavern pillars; on the swell
  The silver lily heaved and fell;
And many a slope was rich in bloom

From him that on the mountain lea
By dancing rivulets fed his flocks,
To him who sat upon the rocks,
And fluted to the morning sea.

SONNET TO W. C. MACREADY

Farewell, Macready, since to-night we part;
Full-handed thunders often have confessed
Thy power, well-used to move the public breast.
We thank thee with our voice, and from the heart.
Farewell, Macready, since this night we part.
Go, take thine honours home; rank with the best,
Garrick and statelier Kemble, and the rest
Who made a nation purer through their art.
Thine is it that our drama did not die,
Nor flicker down to brainless pantomime,
And those gilt gauds men-children swarm to see.
Farewell, Macready; moral, grave, sublime;
Our Shakespeare's bland and universal eye
Dwells pleased, through twice a hundred years, on thee.

TO J. W. BLAKESLEY

Clear-headed friend, whose joyful scorn,
Edged with sharp laughter, cuts atwain
The knots that tangle human creeds,
The wounding cords that bind and strain
The heart until it bleeds,
Ray-fringed eyelids of the morn
Roof not a glance so keen as thine:
If aught of prophecy be mine,
Thou wilt not live in vain.

Low-cowering shall the Sophist sit;
Falsehood shall bare her plaited brow:
Fair-fronted Truth shall droop not now
With shrilling shafts of subtle wit.
Nor martyr-flames, nor trenchant swords
Can do away that ancient lie;
A gentler death shall Falsehood die
Shot through and through with cunning words.

Weak Truth a-leaning on her crutch
Wan, wasted Truth in her utmost need,
Thy kingly intellect shall feed,
Until she be an athlete bold,
And weary with a finger's touch
Those writhed limbs of lightning speed;

Like that strange angel which of old,
Until the breaking of the light,
Wrestled with wandering Israel,
Past Yabbok brook the livelong night,
And heaven's mazèd signs stood still
In the dim tract of Penuel.

MINE HOST

Yon huddled cloud his motion shifts,
Where, by the tavern on the dale,
The thirsty horseman, nodding, lifts
The creaming horn of corny ale.

Mellowing, like some old cucumber
That curves and fattens on its bed,
From his own vats, right jolly fare,
Full thirty suns mine host hath fed.

His tavern is our chief resort,
For he, whose cellar is his pride,
Gives stouter ale and riper port
Than any in the countryside.

Mine host is fat, and grey, and wise,
He strokes his beard before he speaks;
And when he laughs, his little eyes
Are swallowed in his pampered cheeks.

He brims his beaker to the top,
With jokes you never heard before,
And sometimes with a twinkling drop
For those who will not taste it more.

A CHARACTER

With a half-glance upon the sky
At night he said, 'The wanderings
Of this most intricate Universe
Teach me the nothingness of things.'
Yet could not all creation pierce
Beyond the bottom of his eye.

He spake of beauty: that the dull
Saw no divinity in grass,
Life in dead stones, or spirit in air;
Then looking as 'twere in a glass,
He smoothed his chin and sleeked his hair,
And said the earth was beautiful.

He spake of virtue: not the gods
More purely, when they wish to charm
Pallas and Juno sitting by:
And with a sweeping of the arm,
And a lack-lustre dead-blue eye,
Devolved his rounded periods.

Most delicately hour by hour
He canvassed human mysteries
And trod on silk, as if the winds
Blew his own praises in his eyes,
And stood aloof from other minds
In impotence of fancied power.

With lips depressed as he were meek,
Himself unto himself he sold:
Upon himself himself did feed:
Quiet, dispassionate, and cold,
And other than his form of creed,
With chiselled features clear and sleek.

TO J. S.

The wind, that beats the mountain, blows
More softly round the open wold,
And gently comes the world to those
That are cast in gentle mould.

And me this knowledge bolder made,
Or else I had not dared to flow
In these words toward you, and invade
Even with a verse your holy woe.

'Tis strange that those we lean on most,
Those in whose laps our limbs are nursed,
Fall into shadow, soonest lost:
Those we love first are taken first.

God gives us love. Something to love
He lends us; but, when love is grown
To ripeness, that on which it throve
Falls off, and love is left alone.

This is the curse of time. Alas!
In grief I am not all unlearned:
Once through mine own doors Death did pass;
One went, who never hath returned.

He will not smile – not speak to me
Once more. Two years his chair is seen
Empty before us. That was he
Without whose life I had not been.

Your loss is rarer; for this star
Rose with you through a little arc
Of heaven, nor having wandered far
Shot on the sudden into dark.

I knew your brother: his mute dust
I honour and his living worth:
A man more pure and bold and just
Was never born into the earth.

I have not looked upon you nigh,
Since that dear soul hath fall'n asleep.
Great Nature is more wise than I:
I will not tell you not to weep.

And though mine own eyes fill with dew,
Drawn from the spirit through the brain,
I will not even preach to you,
'Weep, weeping dulls the inward pain.'

Let Grief be her own mistress still.
    She loveth her own anguish deep
More than much pleasure. Let her will
    Be done – to weep or not to weep

I will not say 'God's ordinance
    Of Death is blown in every wind;'
For that is not a common chance
    That takes away a noble mind.

His memory long, will live alone
    In all our hearts, as mournful light
That broods above the fallen sun,
    And dwells in heaven half the night.

Vain solace! Memory standing near
    Cast down her eyes, and in her throat
Her voice seemed distant, and a tear
    Dropt on the letters as I wrote.

I wrote I know not what. In truth,
    How *should* I soothe you anyway,
Who miss the brother of your youth?
    Yet something I did wish to say:

For he too was a friend to me:
    Both are my friends, and my true breast
Bleedeth for both; yet it may be
    That only silence suiteth best.

Words weaker than your grief would make
    Grief more. 'Twere better I should cease;
Although myself could almost take
    The place of him that sleeps in peace.

Sleep sweetly, tender heart, in peace:
    Sleep, holy spirit, blessèd soul,
While the stars burn, the moons increase,
    And the great ages onward roll.

Sleep till the end, true soul and sweet.
    Nothing comes to thee new or strange.
Sleep full of rest from head to feet;
    Lie still, dry dust, secure of change.

FRATER AVE ATQUE VALE

Row us out from Desenzano, to your Sirmione row!
So they rowed, and there we landed – 'O venusta
        Sirmio!'
There to me through all the groves of olive
        in the summer glow,
There beneath the Roman ruin where the purple
        flowers grow,
Came that 'Ave atque Vale' of the Poet's hopeless woe,
Tenderest of Roman poets nineteen-hundred years ago,
'Frater Ave atque Vale' – as we wandered to and fro
Gazing at the Lydian laughter of the Garda Lake below
Sweet Catullus's all-but-island, olive-silvery Sirmio!

PREFATORY POEM TO MY BROTHER'S SONNETS

Midnight, June 30, 1879

I

Midnight – in no midsummer tune
The breakers lash the shores:
The cuckoo of a joyless June
Is calling out of doors:

And thou hast vanished from thine own
To that which looks like rest,
True brother, only to be known
By those who love thee best.

II

Midnight – and joyless June gone by,
And from the deluged park
The cuckoo of a worse July
Is calling through the dark:

But thou art silent underground,
And o'er thee streams the rain,
True poet, surely to be found
When Truth is found again.

III

And, now to these unsummered skies
The summer bird is still,
Far off a phantom cuckoo cries
From out a phantom hill;

And through this midnight breaks the sun
Of sixty years away,
The light of days when life begun,
The days that seem today,

When all my griefs were shared with thee,
As all my hopes were thine –
As all thou wert was one with me,
May all thou art be mine!

ON HIS STILLBORN SON

Little bosom not yet cold,
Noble forehead made for thought,
Little hands of mighty mould
Clenched as in the fight which they had fought.
He had done battle to be born,
But some brute force of Nature had prevailed
And the little warrior failed.
Whate'er thou wert, whate'er thou art,
Whose life was ended ere thy breath begun,
Thou nine-months neighbour of my dear one's heart,
And howsoe'er thou liest blind and mute,
Thou lookest bold and resolute,
God bless thee dearest son.

From THE LOTOS-EATERS: CHORIC SONG

I

There is sweet music here that softer falls
Than petals from blown roses on the grass,
Or night-dews on still waters between walls
Of shadowy granite, in a gleaming pass;
Music that gentlier on the spirit lies,
Than tired eyelids upon tired eyes;
Music that brings sweet sleep down from
the blissful skies.
Here are cool mosses deep,
And through the moss the ivies creep,
And in the stream the long-leaved flowers weep,
And from the craggy ledge the poppy hangs in sleep.

II

Why are we weighed upon with heaviness,
And utterly consumed with sharp distress,
While all things else have rest from weariness?
All things have rest: why should we toil alone,
We only toil, who are the first of things,
And make perpetual moan,
Still from one sorrow to another thrown:
Nor ever fold our wings,
And cease from wanderings,
Nor steep our brows in slumber's holy balm;

Nor hearken what the inner spirit sings,
'There is no joy but calm!'
Why should we only toil, the roof and crown of things?

III

Lo! in the middle of the wood,
The folded leaf is wooed from out the bud
With winds upon the branch, and there
Grows green and broad, and takes no care,
Sun-steeped at noon, and in the moon
Nightly dew-fed; and turning yellow
Falls, and floats adown the air.
Lo! sweetened with the summer light,
The full-juiced apple, waxing over-mellow,
Drops in a silent autumn night.
All its allotted length of days,
The flower ripens in its place,
Ripens and fades, and falls, and hath no toil,
Fast-rooted in the fruitful soil.

IV

Hateful is the dark-blue sky,
Vaulted o'er the dark-blue sea.
Death is the end of life; ah, why
Should life all labour be?
Let us alone. Time driveth onward fast,
And in a little while our lips are dumb.

Let us alone. What is it that will last?
All things are taken from us, and become
Portions and parcels of the dreadful Past.
Let us alone. What pleasure can we have
To war with evil? Is there any peace
In ever climbing up the climbing wave?
All things have rest, and ripen toward the grave
In silence; ripen, fall and cease:
Give us long rest or death, dark death,
    or dreamful ease.

V

How sweet it were, hearing the downward stream,
With half-shut eyes ever to seem
Falling asleep in a half-dream!
To dream and dream, like yonder amber light,
Which will not leave the myrrh-bush on the height;
To hear each other's whispered speech;
Eating the Lotos day by day,
To watch the crisping ripples on the beach,
And tender curving lines of creamy spray;
To lend our hearts and spirits wholly
To the influence of mild-minded melancholy;
To muse and brood and live again in memory,
With those old faces of our infancy
Heaped over with a mound of grass,
Two handfuls of white dust, shut in an urn of brass!

VI

Dear is the memory of our wedded lives,
And dear the last embraces of our wives
And their warm tears: but all hath suffered change;
For surely now our household hearths are cold:
Our sons inherit us: our looks are strange:
And we should come like ghosts to trouble joy.
Or else the island princes over-bold
Have eat our substance, and the minstrel sings
Before them of the ten-years' war in Troy,
And our great deeds, as half-forgotten things.
Is there confusion in the little isle?
Let what is broken so remain.
The Gods are hard to reconcile:
'Tis hard to settle order once again.
There is confusion worse than death,
Trouble on trouble, pain on pain,
Long labour unto agèd breath,
Sore task to hearts worn out with many wars
And eyes grown dim with gazing on the pilot-stars.

VII

But, propt on beds of amaranth and moly,
How sweet (while warm airs lull us, blowing lowly)
With half-dropt eyelids still,
Beneath a heaven dark and holy,
To watch the long bright river drawing slowly

His waters from the purple hill –
To hear the dewy echoes calling
From cave to cave through the thick-twined vine –
To watch the emerald-coloured water falling
Through many a wov'n acanthus-wreath divine!
Only to hear and see the far-off sparkling brine,
Only to hear were sweet, stretched out beneath
the pine.

VIII

The Lotos blooms below the barren peak:
The Lotos blows by every winding creek:
All day the wind breathes low with mellower tone:
Through every hollow cave and alley lone
Round and round the spicy downs the yellow
Lotos-dust is blown.
We have had enough of action, and of motion we,
Rolled to starboard, rolled to larboard, when the surge
was seething free,
Where the wallowing monster spouted his foam-
fountains in the sea.
Let us swear an oath, and keep it with an equal mind,
In the hollow Lotos-land to live and lie reclined
On the hills like Gods together, careless of mankind.
For they lie beside their nectar, and the bolts are hurled
Far below them in the valleys, and the clouds are
lightly curled

Round their golden houses, girdled with the gleaming
world:
Where they smile in secret, looking over wasted lands,
Blight and famine, plague and earthquake, roaring
deeps and fiery sands,
Clanging fights, and flaming towns, and sinking ships,
and praying hands.
But they smile, they find a music centred in
a doleful song
Steaming up, a lamentation and an ancient tale
of wrong,
Like a tale of little meaning though the words
are strong;
Chanted from an ill-used race of men that cleave
the soil,
Sow the seed, and reap the harvest with enduring toil,
Storing yearly little dues of wheat, and wine and oil;
Till they perish and they suffer – some, 'tis whispered –
down in hell
Suffer endless anguish, others in Elysian valleys dwell,
Resting weary limbs at last on beds of asphodel.
Surely, surely, slumber is more sweet than toil,
the shore
Than labour in the deep mid-ocean, wind and wave
and oar;
Oh rest ye, brother mariners, we will not wander more.

NARRATIVE POEMS

THE LADY OF SHALOTT

I

On either side the river lie
Long fields of barley and of rye,
That clothe the wold and meet the sky;
And through the field the road runs by
        To many-towered Camelot;
And up and down the people go,
Gazing where the lilies blow
Round an island there below,
        The island of Shalott.

Willows whiten, aspens quiver,
Little breezes dusk and shiver
Through the wave that runs for ever
By the island in the river
        Flowing down to Camelot.
Four grey walls, and four grey towers,
Overlook a space of flowers,
And the silent isle imbowers
        The Lady of Shalott.

By the margin, willow-veiled,
Slide the heavy barges trailed
By slow horses; and unhailed
The shallop flitteth silken-sailed
        Skimming down to Camelot:

But who hath seen her wave her hand?
Or at the casement seen her stand?
Or is she known in all the land
The Lady of Shalott?

Only reapers, reaping early
In among the bearded barley,
Hear a song that echoes cheerly
From the river winding clearly,
Down to towered Camelot:
And by the moon the reaper weary,
Piling sheaves in uplands airy,
Listening, whispers ''Tis the fairy
Lady of Shalott.'

II

There she weaves by night and day
A magic web with colours gay.
She has heard a whisper say,
A curse is on her if she stay
To look down to Camelot.
She knows not what the curse may be,
And so she weaveth steadily,
And little other care hath she,
The Lady of Shalott.

And moving through a mirror clear
That hangs before her all the year

Shadows of the world appear.
There she sees the highway near
Winding down to Camelot:
There the river eddy whirls
And there the surly village-churls,
And the red cloaks of market girls
Pass onward from Shalott.

Sometimes a troop of damsels glad,
An abbot on an ambling pad,
Sometimes a curly shepherd-lad,
Or long-haired page in crimson clad,
Goes by to towered Camelot;
And sometimes through the mirror blue
The knights come riding two and two:
She hath no loyal knight and true,
The Lady of Shalott.

But in her web she still delights
To weave the mirror's magic sights,
For often through the silent nights
A funeral, with plumes and lights
And music, went to Camelot:
Or when the moon was overhead,
Came two young lovers lately wed.
'I am half sick of shadows,' said
The Lady of Shalott.

III

A bow-shot from her bower-eaves,
He rode between the barley-sheaves,
The sun came dazzling through the leaves
And flamed upon the brazen greaves
Of bold Sir Lancelot.
A red-cross knight for ever kneeled
To a lady in his shield
That sparkled on the yellow field,
Beside remote Shalott.

The gemmy bridle glittered free,
Like to some branch of stars we see
Hung in the golden Galaxy.
The bridle bells rang merrily
As he rode down to Camelot:
And from his blazoned baldric slung
A mighty silver bugle hung,
And as he rode his armour rung,
Beside remote Shalott.

All in the blue unclouded weather
Thick-jewelled shone the saddle-leather,
The helmet and the helmet-feather
Burned like one burning flame together,
As he rode down to Camelot.
As often through the purple night,
Below the starry clusters bright,

Some bearded meteor, trailing light,
Moves over still Shalott.

His broad clear brow in sunlight glowed;
On burnished hooves his war-horse trode;
From underneath his helmet flowed
His coal-black curls as on he rode
As he rode down to Camelot.
From the bank and from the river
He flashed into the crystal mirror,
'Tirra lirra,' by the river
Sang Sir Lancelot.

She left the web, she left the loom,
She made three paces through the room,
She saw the water-lily bloom,
She saw the helmet and the plume,
She looked down to Camelot.
Out flew the web and floated wide;
The mirror cracked from side to side;
'The curse is come upon me,' cried
The Lady of Shalott.

IV

In the stormy east-wind straining,
The pale yellow woods were waning,
The broad stream in his banks complaining,
Heavily the low sky raining

Over towered Camelot;
Down she came and found a boat
Beneath a willow left afloat,
And round about the prow she wrote
The Lady of Shalott.

And down the river's dim expanse –
Like some bold seër in a trance,
Seeing all his own mischance –
With a glassy countenance
Did she look to Camelot.
And at the closing of the day
She loosed the chain, and down she lay;
The broad stream bore her far away,
The Lady of Shalott.

Lying robed in snowy white
That loosely flew to left and right –
The leaves upon her falling light –
Through the noises of the night
She floated down to Camelot:
And as the boat-head wound along
The willowy hills and fields among,
They heard her singing her last song,
The Lady of Shalott.

Heard a carol, mournful, holy
Chanted loudly, chanted lowly,

Till her blood was frozen slowly,
And her eyes were darkened wholly,
Turned to towered Camelot.
For ere she reached upon the tide
The first house by the water-side,
Singing in her song she died,
The Lady of Shalott.

Under tower and balcony,
By garden-wall and gallery,
A gleaming shape she floated by,
Dead-pale between the houses high,
Silent into Camelot.
Out upon the wharfs they came,
Knight and burgher, lord and dame,
And round the prow they read her name,
The Lady of Shalott.

Who is this? and what is here?
And in the lighted palace near
Died the sound of royal cheer;
And they crossed themselves for fear,
All the knights at Camelot:
But Lancelot mused a little space;
He said, 'She has a lovely face;
God in his mercy lend her grace,
The Lady of Shalott.'

ULYSSES

It little profits that an idle king,
By this still hearth, among these barren crags,
Matched with an agèd wife, I mete and dole
Unequal laws unto a savage race,
That hoard, and sleep, and feed, and know not me.

I cannot rest from travel: I will drink
Life to the lees: all times I have enjoyed
Greatly, have suffered greatly, both with those
That loved me, and alone; on shore, and when
Through scudding drifts the rainy Hyades
Vext the dim sea: I am become a name;
For always roaming with a hungry heart
Much have I seen and known; cities of men
And manners, climates, councils, governments,
Myself not least, but honoured of them all;
And drunk delight of battle with my peers,
Far on the ringing plains of windy Troy.
I am a part of all that I have met;
Yet all experience is an arch wherethrough
Gleams that untravelled world, whose margin fades
For ever and for ever when I move.
How dull it is to pause, to make an end,
To rust unburnished, not to shine in use!
As though to breathe were life. Life piled on life

Were all too little, and of one to me
Little remains: but every hour is saved
From that eternal silence, something more,
A bringer of new things; and vile it were
For some three suns to store and hoard myself,
And this grey spirit yearning in desire
To follow knowledge, like a sinking star,
Beyond the utmost bound of human thought.

This is my son, mine own Telemachus,
To whom I leave the sceptre and the isle –
Well-loved of me, discerning to fulfil
This labour, by slow prudence to make mild
A rugged people, and through soft degrees
Subdue them to the useful and the good.
Most blameless is he, centred in the sphere
Of common duties, decent not to fail
In offices of tenderness, and pay
Meet adoration to my household gods,
When I am gone. He works his work, I mine.

There lies the port: the vessel puffs her sail:
There gloom the dark broad seas. My mariners,
Souls that have toiled, and wrought, and thought
with me –
That ever with a frolic welcome took
The thunder and the sunshine, and opposed

Free hearts, free foreheads – you and I are old;
Old age hath yet his honour and his toil;
Death closes all: but something ere the end,
Some work of noble note, may yet be done,
Not unbecoming men that strove with Gods.
The lights begin to twinkle from the rocks:
The long day wanes: the slow moon climbs: the deep
Moans round with many voices. Come, my friends,
'Tis not too late to seek a newer world.
Push off, and sitting well in order smite
The sounding furrows; for my purpose holds
To sail beyond the sunset, and the baths
Of all the western stars, until I die.
It may be that the gulfs will wash us down:
It may be we shall touch the Happy Isles,
And see the great Achilles, whom we knew.
Though much is taken, much abides; and though
We are not now that strength which in old days
Moved earth and heaven; that which we are, we are;
One equal temper of heroic hearts,
Made weak by time and fate, but strong in will
To strive, to seek, to find, and not to yield.

TITHONUS

The woods decay, the woods decay and fall,
The vapours weep their burthen to the ground,
Man comes and tills the field and lies beneath,
And after many a summer dies the swan.
Me only cruel immortality
Consumes: I wither slowly in thine arms,
Here at the quiet limit of the world,
A white-haired shadow roaming like a dream
The ever-silent spaces of the East,
Far-folded mists, and gleaming halls of morn.

Alas! for this grey shadow, once a man –
So glorious in his beauty and thy choice,
Who madest him thy chosen, that he seemed
To his great heart none other than a God!
I asked thee, 'Give me immortality.'
Then didst thou grant mine asking with a smile,
Like wealthy men who care not how they give.
But thy strong Hours indignant worked their wills,
And beat me down and marred and wasted me,
And though they could not end me, left me maimed
To dwell in presence of immortal youth,
Immortal age beside immortal youth,
And all I was, in ashes. Can thy love,
Thy beauty, make amends, though even now,

Close over us, the silver star, thy guide,
Shines in those tremulous eyes that fill with tears
To hear me? Let me go: take back thy gift:
Why should a man desire in any way
To vary from the kindly race of men,
Or pass beyond the goal of ordinance
Where all should pause, as is most meet for all?

A soft air fans the cloud apart; there comes
A glimpse of that dark world where I was born.
Once more the old mysterious glimmer steals
From thy pure brows, and from thy shoulders pure,
And bosom beating with a heart renewed.
Thy cheek begins to redden through the gloom,
Thy sweet eyes brighten slowly close to mine,
Ere yet they blind the stars, and the wild team
Which love thee, yearning for thy yoke, arise,
And shake the darkness from their loosened manes,
And beat the twilight into flakes of fire.

Lo! ever thus thou growest beautiful
In silence, then before thine answer given
Departest, and thy tears are on my cheek.

Why wilt thou ever scare me with thy tears,
And make me tremble lest a saying learnt,
In days far-off, on that dark earth, be true?
'The Gods themselves cannot recall their gifts.'

Ay me! ay me! with what another heart
In days far-off, and with what other eyes
I used to watch – if I be he that watched –
The lucid outline forming round thee; saw
The dim curls kindle into sunny rings;
Changed with thy mystic change, and felt my blood
Glow with the glow that slowly crimsoned all
Thy presence and thy portals, while I lay,
Mouth, forehead, eyelids, growing dewy-warm
With kisses balmier than half-opening buds
Of April, and could hear the lips that kissed
Whispering I knew not what of wild and sweet,
Like that strange song I heard Apollo sing,
While Ilion like a mist rose into towers.

Yet hold me not for ever in thine East:
How can my nature longer mix with thine?
Coldly thy rosy shadows bathe me, cold
Are all thy lights, and cold my wrinkled feet
Upon thy glimmering thresholds, when the steam
Floats up from those dim fields about the homes
Of happy men that have the power to die,
And grassy barrows of the happier dead.
Release me, and restore me to the ground;
Thou seëst all things, thou wilt see my grave:
Thou wilt renew thy beauty morn by morn;
I earth in earth forget these empty courts,
And thee returning on thy silver wheels.

THE EPIC

At Francis Allen's on the Christmas-eve –
The game of forfeits done – the girls all kissed
Beneath the sacred bush and past away –
The parson Holmes, the poet Everard Hall,
The host, and I sat round the wassail-bowl,
Then half-way ebbed: and there we held a talk,
How all the old honour had from Christmas gone,
Or gone, or dwindled down to some odd games
In some odd nooks like this; till I, tired out
With cutting eights that day upon the pond,
Where, three times slipping from the outer edge,
I bumped the ice into three several stars,
Fell in a doze; and half-awake I heard
The parson taking wide and wider sweeps,
Now harping on the church-commissioners,
Now hawking at Geology and schism;
Until I woke, and found him settled down
Upon the general decay of faith
Right through the world, 'at home was little left,
And none abroad: there was no anchor, none,
To hold by.' Francis, laughing, clapt his hand
On Everard's shoulder, with 'I hold by him.'
'And I,' quoth Everard, 'by the wassail-bowl.'
'Why yes,' I said, 'we knew your gift that way
At college: but another which you had,

I mean of verse (for so we held it then),
What came of that?' 'You know,' said Frank, 'he burnt
His epic, his King Arthur, some twelve books' –
And then to me demanding why? 'Oh, sir,
He thought that nothing new was said, or else
Something so said 'twas nothing – that a truth
Looks freshest in the fashion of the day:
God knows: he has a mint of reasons: ask.
It pleased me well enough.' 'Nay, nay,' said Hall,
'Why take the style of those heroic times?
For nature brings not back the Mastodon,
Nor we those times; and why should any man
Remodel models? these twelve books of mine
Were faint Homeric echoes, nothing-worth,
Mere chaff and draff, much better burnt.' 'But I,'
Said Francis, 'picked the eleventh from this hearth,
And have it: keep a thing, its use will come.
I hoard it as a sugar-plum for Holmes.'
He laughed, and I, though sleepy, like a horse
That hears the corn-bin open, pricked my ears;
For I remembered Everard's college fame
When we were Freshmen: then at my request
He brought it; and the poet little urged,
But with some prelude of disparagement,
Read, mouthing out his hollow oes and aes,
Deep-chested music, and to this result.

MORTE D'ARTHUR

So all day long the noise of battle rolled
Among the mountains by the winter sea;
Until King Arthur's table, man by man,
Had fallen in Lyonnesse about their Lord,
King Arthur: then, because his wound was deep,
The bold Sir Bedivere uplifted him,
Sir Bedivere, the last of all his knights,
And bore him to a chapel nigh the field,
A broken chancel with a broken cross,
That stood on a dark strait of barren land.
On one side lay the Ocean, and on one
Lay a great water, and the moon was full.
Then spake King Arthur to Sir Bedivere:
'The sequel of to-day unsolders all
The goodliest fellowship of famous knights
Whereof this world holds record. Such a sleep
They sleep – the men I loved. I think that we
Shall never more, at any future time,
Delight our souls with talk of knightly deeds,
Walking about the gardens and the halls
Of Camelot, as in the days that were.
I perish by this people which I made, –
Though Merlin sware that I should come again
To rule once more – but let what will be, be,
I am so deeply smitten through the helm

That without help I cannot last till morn.
Thou therefore take my brand Excalibur,
Which was my pride: for thou rememberest how
In those old days, one summer noon, an arm
Rose up from out the bosom of the lake,
Clothed in white samite, mystic, wonderful,
Holding the sword – and how I rowed across
And took it, and have worn it, like a king:
And, wheresoever I am sung or told
In aftertime this also shall be known:
But now delay not: take Excalibur,
And fling him far into the middle mere:
Watch what thou seëst, and lightly bring me word.'
To him replied the bold Sir Bedivere:
'It is not meet, Sir King, to leave thee thus,
Aidless, alone, and smitten through the helm.
A little thing may harm a wounded man.
Yet I thy hest will all perform at full,
Watch what I see, and lightly bring thee word.'
So saying, from the ruined shrine he stept
And in the moon athwart the place of tombs,
Where lay the mighty bones of ancient men,
Old knights, and over them the sea-wind sang
Shrill, chill, with flakes of foam. He, stepping down
By zig-zag paths, and juts of pointed rock,
Came on the shining levels of the lake.
There drew he forth the brand Excalibur,

And o'er him, drawing it, the winter moon,
Brightening the skirts of a long cloud, ran forth
And sparkled keen with frost against the hilt:
For all the haft twinkled with diamond sparks,
Myriads of topaz-lights, and jacinth-work
Of subtlest jewellery. He gazed so long
That both his eyes were dazzled, as he stood,
This way and that dividing the swift mind,
In act to throw: but at the last it seemed
Better to leave Excalibur concealed
There in the many-knotted waterflags,
That whistled stiff and dry about the marge.
So strode he back slow to the wounded King.
  Then spake King Arthur to Sir Bedivere:
'Hast thou performed my mission which I gave?
What is it thou hast seen? or what hast heard?'
  And answer made the bold Sir Bedivere:
'I heard the ripple washing in the reeds,
And the wild water lapping on the crag.'
  To whom replied King Arthur, faint and pale:
'Thou hast betrayed thy nature and thy name,
Not rendering true answer, as beseemed
Thy fëalty, nor like a noble knight:
For surer sign had followed, either hand,
Or voice, or else a motion of the mere.
This is a shameful thing for men to lie.
Yet now, I charge thee, quickly go again

As thou art lief and dear, and do the thing
I bad thee, watch, and lightly bring me word.'
  Then went Sir Bedivere the second time
Across the ridge, and paced beside the mere,
Counting the dewy pebbles, fixed in thought;
But when he saw the wonder of the hilt,
How curiously and strangely chased, he smote
His palms together, and he cried aloud,
  'And if indeed I cast the brand away,
Surely a precious thing, one worthy note,
Should thus be lost for ever from the earth,
Which might have pleased the eyes of many men.
What good should follow this, if this were done?
What harm, undone? deep harm to disobey,
Seeing obedience is the bond of rule.
Were it well to obey then, if a king demand
An act unprofitable, against himself?
The King is sick, and knows not what he does.
What record, or what relic of my lord
Should be to aftertime, but empty breath
And rumours of a doubt? but were this kept,
Stored in some treasure-house of mighty kings,
Some one might show it at a joust of arms,
Saying, "King Arthur's sword, Excalibur
Wrought by the lonely maiden of the Lake.
Nine years she wrought it, sitting in the deeps
Upon the hidden bases of the hills."

So might some old man speak in the aftertime
To all the people, winning reverence.
But now much honour and much fame were lost.'
  So spake he, clouded with his own conceit,
And hid Excalibur the second time,
And so strode back slow to the wounded King.
  Then spoke King Arthur, breathing heavily:
'What is it thou hast seen? or what hast heard?'
  And answer made the bold Sir Bedivere:
'I heard the water lapping on the crag,
And the long ripple washing in the reeds.'
  To whom replied King Arthur, much in wrath:
'Ah, miserable and unkind, untrue,
Unknightly, traitor-hearted! Woe is me!
Authority forgets a dying king,
Laid widowed of the power in his eye
That bowed the will. I see thee what thou art,
For thou, the latest-left of all my knights,
In whom should meet the offices of all,
Thou wouldst betray me for the precious hilt;
Either from lust of gold, or like a girl
Valuing the giddy pleasure of the eyes.
Yet, for a man may fail in duty twice,
And the third time may prosper, get thee hence:
But, if thou spare to fling Excalibur,
I will arise and slay thee with my hands.'
  Then quickly rose Sir Bedivere, and ran,

And, leaping down the ridges lightly, plunged
Among the bulrush-beds, and clutched the sword,
And strongly wheeled and threw it. The great brand
Made lightnings in the splendour of the moon,
And flashing round and round, and whirled in an arch,
Shot like a streamer of the northern morn,
Seen where the moving isles of winter shock
By night, with noises of the northern sea.
So flashed and fell the brand Excalibur:
But ere he dipt the surface, rose an arm
Clothed in white samite, mystic, wonderful,
And caught him by the hilt, and brandished him
Three times, and drew him under in the mere.
And lightly went the other to the King.
   Then spoke King Arthur, drawing thicker breath:
'Now see I by thine eyes that this is done.
Speak out: what is it thou hast heard, or seen?'
   And answer made the bold Sir Bedivere:
'Sir King, I closed mine eyelids, lest the gems
Should blind my purpose, for I never saw,
Nor shall see, here or elsewhere, till I die,
Not though I live three lives of mortal men,
So great a miracle as yonder hilt.
Then with both hands I flung him, wheeling him;
But when I looked again, behold an arm,
Clothed in white samite, mystic, wonderful,
That caught him by the hilt, and brandished him

Three times, and drew him under in the mere.'
And answer made King Arthur, breathing hard:
'My end draws nigh; 'tis time that I were gone.
Make broad thy shoulders to receive my weight,
And bear me to the margin; yet I fear
My wound hath taken cold, and I shall die.'
So saying, from the pavement he half rose,
Slowly, with pain, reclining on his arm,
And looking wistfully with wide blue eyes
As in a picture. Him Sir Bedivere
Remorsefully regarded through his tears,
And would have spoken, but he found not words,
Then took with care, and kneeling on one knee,
O'er both his shoulders drew the languid hands,
And rising bore him through the place of tombs.
But, as he walked, King Arthur panted hard,
Like one that feels a nightmare on his bed
When all the house is mute. So sighed the King,
Muttering and murmuring at his ear, 'Quick, quick!
I fear it is too late, and I shall die.'
But the other swiftly strode from ridge to ridge,
Clothed with his breath, and looking, as he walked,
Larger than human on the frozen hills.
He heard the deep behind him, and a cry
Before. His own thought drove him like a goad.
Dry clashed his harness in the icy caves
And barren chasms, and all to left and right

The bare black cliff clanged round him, as he based
His feet on juts of slippery crag that rang
Sharp-smitten with the dint of armèd heels –
And on a sudden, lo! the level lake,
And the long glories of the winter moon.
  Then saw they how there hove a dusky barge,
Dark as a funeral scarf from stem to stern,
Beneath them; and descending they were ware
That all the decks were dense with stately forms
Black-stoled, black-hooded, like a dream – by these
Three Queens with crowns of gold – and from
    them rose
A cry that shivered to the tingling stars,
And, as it were one voice, an agony
Of lamentation, like a wind, that shrills
All night in a waste land, where no one comes,
Or hath come, since the making of the world.
  Then murmured Arthur, 'Place me in the barge,'
And to the barge they came. There those three Queens
Put forth their hands, and took the King, and wept.
But she, that rose the tallest of them all
And fairest, laid his head upon her lap,
And loosed the shattered casque, and chafed his hands,
And called him by his name, complaining loud,
And dropping bitter tears against his brow
Striped with dark blood: for all his face was white
And colourless, and like the withered moon

Smote by the fresh beam of the springing east;
And all his greaves and cuisses dashed with drops
Of onset; and the light and lustrous curls –
That made his forehead like a rising sun
High from the dais-throne – were parched with dust;
Or, clotted into points and hanging loose,
Mixed with the knightly growth that fringed his lips.
So like a shattered column lay the King;
Not like that Arthur who, with lance in rest,
From spur to plume a star of tournament,
Shot through the lists at Camelot, and charged
Before the eyes of ladies and of kings.
  Then loudly cried the bold Sir Bedivere,
'Ah! my Lord Arthur, whither shall I go?
Where shall I hide my forehead and my eyes?
For now I see the true old times are dead,
When every morning brought a noble chance,
And every chance brought out a noble knight.
Such times have been not since the light that led
The holy Elders with the gift of myrrh.
But now the whole ROUND TABLE is dissolved
Which was an image of the mighty world;
And I, the last, go forth companionless,
And the days darken round me, and the years,
Among new men, strange faces, other minds.'
  And slowly answered Arthur from the barge:
'The old order changeth, yielding place to new,

And God fulfils Himself in many ways,
Lest one good custom should corrupt the world.
Comfort thyself: what comfort is in me?
I have lived my life, and that which I have done
May He within Himself make pure! but thou,
If thou shouldst never see my face again,
Pray for my soul. More things are wrought by prayer
Than this world dreams of. Wherefore, let thy voice
Rise like a fountain for me night and day.
For what are men better than sheep or goats
That nourish a blind life within the brain,
If, knowing God, they lift not hands of prayer
Both for themselves and those who call them friend?
For so the whole round earth is every way
Bound by gold chains about the feet of God.
But now farewell. I am going a long way
With these thou seëst – if indeed I go –
(For all my mind is clouded with a doubt)
To the island-valley of Avilion;
Where falls not hail, or rain, or any snow,
Nor ever wind blows loudly, but it lies
Deep-meadowed, happy, fair with orchard-lawns
And bowery hollows crowned with summer sea,
Where I will heal me of my grievous wound.'

So said he, and the barge with oar and sail
Moved from the brink, like some full-breasted swan
That, fluting a wild carol ere her death,

Ruffles her pure cold plume, and takes the flood
With swarthy webs. Long stood Sir Bedivere
Revolving many memories, till the hull
Looked one black dot against the verge of dawn,
And on the mere the wailing died away.

*

Here ended Hall, and our last light, that long
Had winked and threatened darkness, flared and fell:
At which the Parson, sent to sleep with sound,
And waked with silence, grunted 'Good!' but we
Sat rapt: it was the tone with which he read –
Perhaps some modern touches here and there
Redeemed it from the charge of nothingness –
Or else we loved the man and prized his work;
I know not: but we sitting, as I said,
The cock crew loud; as at that time of year
The lusty bird takes every hour for dawn:
Then Francis, muttering, like a man ill-used,
'There now – that's nothing!' drew a little back,
And drove his heel into the smouldered log,
That sent a blast of sparkles up the flue:
And so to bed; where yet in sleep I seemed
To sail with Arthur under looming shores,
Point after point; till on to dawn, when dreams
Begin to feel the truth and stir of day,
To me, methought, who waited with a crowd,

There came a bark that, blowing forward, bore
King Arthur, like a modern gentleman
Of stateliest port; and all the people cried
'Arthur is come again: he cannot die.'
Then those that stood upon the hills behind
Repeated – 'Come again and thrice as fair;'
And, further inland, voices echoed – 'Come
With all good things, and war shall be no more.'
At this a hundred bells began to peal,
That with the sound I woke, and heard indeed
The clear church-bells ring in the Christmas morn.

ST SIMEON STYLITES

Although I be the basest of mankind,
From scalp to sole one slough and crust of sin,
Unfit for earth, unfit for heaven, scarce meet
For troops of devils, mad with blasphemy,
I will not cease to grasp the hope I hold
Of saintdom, and to clamour, mourn and sob,
Battering the gates of heaven with storms of prayer,
Have mercy, Lord, and take away my sin.

Let this avail, just, dreadful, mighty God,
This not be all in vain, that thrice ten years,
Thrice multiplied by superhuman pangs,
In hungers and in thirsts, fevers and cold,
In coughs, aches, stitches, ulcerous throes and cramps,
A sign betwixt the meadow and the cloud,
Patient on this tall pillar I have borne
Rain, wind, frost, heat, hail, damp, and sleet, and snow;
And I had hoped that ere this period closed
Thou wouldst have caught me up into thy rest,
Denying not these weather-beaten limbs
The meed of saints, the white robe and the palm.

O take the meaning, Lord: I do not breathe,
Not whisper, any murmur of complaint.
Pain heaped ten-hundred-fold to this, were still

Less burthen, by ten-hundred-fold, to bear,
Than were those lead-like tons of sin, that crushed
My spirit flat before thee.
O Lord, Lord,
Thou knowest I bore this better at the first,
For I was strong and hale of body then;
And though my teeth, which now are dropt away,
Would chatter with the cold, and all my beard
Was tagged with icy fringes in the moon,
I drowned the whoopings of the owl with sound
Of pious hymns and psalms, and sometimes saw
An angel stand and watch me, as I sang.
Now am I feeble grown; my end draws nigh;
I hope my end draws nigh: half deaf I am,
So that I scarce can hear the people hum
About the column's base, and almost blind
And scarce can recognize the fields I know,
And both my thighs are rotted with the dew;
Yet cease I not to clamour and to cry,
While my stiff spine can hold my weary head,
Till all my limbs drop piecemeal from the stone,
Have mercy, mercy: take away my sin.

O Jesus, if thou wilt not save my soul,
Who may be saved? who is it may be saved?
Who may be made a saint, if I fail here?
Show me the man hath suffered more than I.

For did not all thy martyrs die one death?
For either they were stoned or crucified
Or burned in fire, or boiled in oil, or sawn
In twain beneath the ribs; but I die here
To-day, and whole years long, a life of death.
Bear witness, if I could have found a way
(And heedfully I sifted all my thought)
More slowly-painful to subdue this home
Of sin, my flesh, which I despise and hate,
I had not stinted practice, O my God.

For not alone this pillar-punishment,
Not this alone I bore: but while I lived
In the white convent down the valley there,
For many weeks about my loins I wore
The rope that haled the buckets from the well,
Twisted as tight as I could knot the noose;
And spake not of it to a single soul,
Until the ulcer, eating through my skin,
Betrayed my secret penance, so that all
My brethren marvelled greatly. More than this
I bore, whereof, O God, thou knowest all.

Three winters, that my soul might grow to thee,
I lived up there on yonder mountain side.
My right leg chained into the crag, I lay
Pent in a roofless close of ragged stones;

Inswathed sometimes in wandering mist, and twice
Blacked with thy branding thunder, and sometimes
Sucking the damps for drink, and eating not,
Except the spare chance-gift of those that came
To touch my body and be healed, and live:
And they say then that I worked miracles,
Whereof my fame is loud amongst mankind,
Cured lameness, palsies, cancers. Thou, O God,
Knowest alone whether this was or no.
Have mercy, mercy; cover all my sin.

Then, that I might be more alone with thee,
Three years I lived upon a pillar, high
Six cubits, and three years on one of twelve;
And twice three years I crouched on one that rose
Twenty by measure; last of all, I grew
Twice ten long weary weary years to this,
That numbers forty cubits from the soil.

I think that I have borne as much as this –
Or else I dream – and for so long a time,
If I may measure time by yon slow light,
And this high dial, which my sorrow crowns –
So much – even so.

And yet I know not well,
For that the evil ones come here, and say,
'Fall down, O Simeon: thou hast suffered long

For ages and for ages!' then they prate
Of penances I cannot have gone through,
Perplexing me with lies; and oft I fall,
Maybe for months, in such blind lethargies
That Heaven, and Earth, and Time are choked.

But yet

Bethink thee, Lord, while thou and all the saints
Enjoy themselves in heaven, and men on earth
House in the shade of comfortable roofs
Sit with their wives by fires, eat wholesome food
And wear warm clothes, and even beasts have stalls,
I, 'tween the spring and downfall of the light
Bow down one thousand and two hundred times,
To Christ, the Virgin Mother, and the Saints;
Or in the night, after a little sleep,
I wake: the chill stars sparkle; I am wet
With drenching dews, or stiff with crackling frost.
I wear an undressed goatskin on my back;
A grazing iron collar grinds my neck;
And in my weak, lean arms I lift the cross,
And strive and wrestle with thee till I die:
O mercy, mercy! wash away my sin.

O Lord, thou knowest what a man I am;
A sinful man, conceived and born in sin:
'Tis their own doing; this is none of mine;
Lay it not to me. Am I to blame for this,

That here come those that worship me? Ha! ha!
They think that I am somewhat. What am I?
The silly people take me for a saint,
And bring me offerings of fruit and flowers:
And I, in truth (thou wilt bear witness here)
Have all in all endured as much, and more
Than many just and holy men, whose names
Are registered and calendared for saints.

Good people, you do ill to kneel to me.
What is it I can have done to merit this?
I am a sinner viler than you all.
It may be I have wrought some miracles
And cured some halt and maimed, but what of that?
It may be, no one, even among the saints,
May match his pains with mine; but what of that?
Yet do not rise: for you may look on me,
And in your looking you may kneel to God.
Speak! is there any of you halt or maimed?
I think you know I have some power with Heaven
From my long penance: let him speak his wish.

Yes, I can heal him. Power goes forth from me.
They say that they are healed. Ah, hark! they shout
'St Simeon Stylites.' Why, if so,
God reaps a harvest in me. O my soul,
God reaps a harvest in thee. If this be,

Can I work miracles and not be saved?
This is not told of any. They were saints.
It cannot be but that I shall be saved;
Yea, crowned a saint. They shout, 'Behold a saint!',
And lower voices saint me from above.
Courage, St Simeon! This dull chrysalis
Cracks into shining wings, and hope ere death
Spreads more and more and more, that God hath now
Sponged and made blank of crimeful record all
My mortal archives.

O my sons, my sons,
I, Simeon of the pillar, by surname
Stylites, among men; I, Simeon,
The watcher on the column till the end;
I, Simeon, whose brain the sunshine bakes;
I, whose bald brows in silent hours become
Unnaturally hoar with rime, do now
From my high nest of penance here proclaim
That Pontius and Iscariot by my side
Showed like fair seraphs. On the coals I lay,
A vessel full of sin: all hell beneath
Made me boil over. Devils plucked my sleeve,
Abaddon and Asmodeus caught at me.
I smote them with the cross; they swarmed again.
In bed like monstrous apes they crushed my chest:
They flapped my light out as I read: I saw
Their faces grow between me and my book;

With colt-like whinny and with hoggish whine
They burst my prayer. Yet this way was left,
And by this way I 'scaped them. Mortify
Your flesh, like me, with scourges and with thorns;
Smite, shrink not, spare not. If it may be, fast
Whole Lents, and pray. I hardly, with slow steps,
With slow, faint steps, and much exceeding pain,
Have scrambled past those pits of fire, that still
Sing in mine ears. But yield not me the praise:
God only through his bounty hath thought fit,
Among the powers and princes of this world,
To make me an example to mankind,
Which few can reach to. Yet I do not say
But that a time may come – yea, even now,
Now, now, his footsteps smite the threshold stairs
Of life – I say, that time is at the doors
When you may worship me without reproach;
For I will leave my relics in your land,
And you may carve a shrine about my dust,
And burn a fragrant lamp before my bones,
When I am gathered to the glorious saints.

While I spake then, a sting of shrewdest pain
Ran shrivelling through me, and a cloudlike change,
In passing, with a grosser film made thick
These heavy, horny eyes. The end! the end!
Surely the end! What's here? a shape, a shade,

A flash of light. Is that the angel there
That holds a crown? Come, blessed brother, come.
I know thy glittering face. I waited long;
My brows are ready. What! deny it now?
Nay, draw, draw, draw nigh. So I clutch it. Christ!
'Tis gone: 'tis here again; the crown! the crown!
So now 'tis fitted on and grows to me,
And from it melt the dews of Paradise,
Sweet! sweet! spikenard, and balm, and frankincense.
Ah! let me not be fooled, sweet saints, I trust:
That I am whole, and clean, and meet for Heaven.

Speak, if there be a priest, a man of God,
Among you there, and let him presently
Approach, and lean a ladder on the shaft,
And climbing up into my airy home,
Deliver me the blessed sacrament;
For by the warning of the Holy Ghost,
I prophesy that I shall die to-night,
A quarter before twelve.
But thou, O Lord,
Aid all this foolish people; let them take
Example, pattern: lead them to thy light.

TO PROFESSOR JEBB, WITH THE FOLLOWING POEM

Fair things are slow to fade away,
Bear witness you, that yesterday
    From out the Ghost of Pindar in you
Rolled an Olympian; and they say

That here the torpid mummy wheat
Of Egypt bore a grain as sweet
    As that which gilds the glebe of England,
Sunned with a summer of milder heat.

So may this legend for awhile,
If greeted by your classic smile,
    Though dead in its Trinacrian Enna,
Blossom again on a colder isle.

DEMETER AND PERSEPHONE

Faint as a climate-changing bird that flies
All night across the darkness, and at dawn
Falls on the threshold of her native land,
And can no more, thou camest, O my child,
Led upward by the God of ghosts and dreams,
Who laid thee at Eleusis, dazed and dumb
With passing through at once from state to state,
Until I brought thee hither, that the day,
When here thy hands let fall the gathered flower,
Might break through clouded memories once again
On thy lost self. A sudden nightingale
Saw thee, and flashed into a frolic of song
And welcome; and a gleam as of the moon,
When first she peers along the tremulous deep,
Fled wavering o'er thy face, and chased away
That shadow of a likeness to the king
Of shadows, thy dark mate. Persephone!
Queen of the dead no more – my child! Thine eyes
Again were human-godlike, and the Sun
Burst from a swimming fleece of winter grey,
And robed thee in his day from head to feet –
'Mother!' and I was folded in thine arms.

Child, those imperial disimpassioned eyes
Awed even me at first, thy mother – eyes

That oft had seen the serpent-wanded power
Draw downward into Hades with his drift
Of flickering spectres, lighted from below
By the red race of fiery Phlegethon;
But when before have Gods or men beheld
The Life that had descended re-arise,
And lighted from above him by the Sun?
So mighty was the mother's childless cry,
A cry that rang through Hades, Earth, and Heaven!

So in this pleasant vale we stand again,
The field of Enna, now once more ablaze
With flowers that brighten as thy footstep falls,
All flowers – but for one black blur of earth
Left by that closing chasm, through which the car
Of dark Aïdoneus rising rapt thee hence.
And here, my child, though folded in thine arms,
I feel the deathless heart of motherhood
Within me shudder, lest the naked glebe
Should yawn once more into the gulf, and thence
The shrilly whinnyings of the team of Hell,
Ascending, pierce the glad and songful air,
And all at once their arched necks, midnight-maned,
Jet upward through the mid-day blossom. No!
For, see, thy foot has touched it; all the space
Of blank earth-baldness clothes itself afresh,
And breaks into the crocus-purple hour

That saw thee vanish.
Child, when thou wert gone,
I envied human wives, and nested birds,
Yea, the cubbed lioness; went in search of thee
Through many a palace, many a cot, and gave
Thy breast to ailing infants in the night,
And set the mother waking in amaze
To find her sick one whole; and forth again
Among the wail of midnight winds, and cried,
'Where is my loved one? Wherefore do ye wail?'
And out from all the night an answer shrilled
'We know not, and we know not why we wail.'
I climbed on all the cliffs of all the seas,
And asked the waves that moan about the world
'Where? do ye make your moaning for my child?'
And round from all the world the voices came
'We know not, and we know not why we moan.'
'Where'? and I stared from every eagle-peak,
I thridded the black heart of all the woods,
I peered through tomb and cave, and in the storms
Of Autumn swept across the city, and heard
The murmur of their temples chanting me,
Me, me, the desolate Mother! 'Where'? – and turned,
And fled by many a waste, forlorn of man,
And grieved for man through all my grief for thee, –
The jungle rooted in his shattered hearth,
The serpent coiled about his broken shaft,

The scorpion crawling over naked skulls; –
I saw the tiger in the ruined fane
Spring from his fallen God, but trace of thee
I saw not; and far on, and, following out
A league of labyrinthine darkness, came
On three grey heads beneath a gleaming rift.
'Where'? and I heard one voice from all the three
'We know not, for we spin the lives of men,
And not of Gods, and know not why we spin!
There is a Fate beyond us.' Nothing knew.

Last as the likeness of a dying man,
Without his knowledge, from him flits to warn
A far-friendship that he comes no more,
So he, the God of dreams, who heard my cry,
Drew from thyself the likeness of thyself
Without thy knowledge, and thy shadow past,
Before me, crying 'The Bright one in the highest
Is brother of the Dark one in the lowest,
And Bright and Dark have sworn that I, the child
Of thee, the great Earth-Mother, thee, the Power
That lifts her buried life from gloom to bloom,
Should be for ever and for evermore
The Bride of Darkness.'

So the Shadow wailed.

Then I, Earth-Goddess, cursed the Gods of Heaven.
I would not mingle with their feasts; to me

Their nectar smacked of hemlock on the lips,
Their rich ambrosia tasted aconite.
The man, that only lives and loves an hour,
Seemed nobler than their hard Eternities.
My quick tears killed the flower, my ravings hushed
The bird, and lost in utter grief I failed
To send my life through olive-yard and vine
And golden grain, my gift to helpless man.
Rain-rotten died the wheat, the barley-spears
Were hollow-husked, the leaf fell, and the sun,
Pale at my grief, drew down before his time
Sickening, and Ætna kept her winter snow.
   Then He, the brother of this Darkness, He
Who still is highest, glancing from his height
On earth a fruitless fallow, when he missed
The wonted steam of sacrifice, the praise
And prayer of men, decreed that thou should'st dwell
For nine white moons of each whole year with me,
Three dark ones in the shadow with thy King.
   Once more the reaper in the gleam of dawn
Will see me by the landmark far away,
Blessing his field, or seated in the dusk
Of even, by the lonely threshing-floor,
Rejoicing in the harvest and the grange.
   Yet I, Earth-Goddess, am but ill-content
With them, who still are highest. Those grey heads,
What meant they by their 'Fate beyond the Fates'

But younger kindlier Gods to bear us down,
As we bore down the Gods before us? Gods,
To quench, not hurl the thunderbolt, to stay,
Not spread the plague, the famine; Gods indeed,
To send the noon into the night and break
The sunless halls of Hades into Heaven?
Till thy dark lord accept and love the Sun,
And all the Shadow die into the Light,
When thou shalt dwell the whole bright year with me,
And souls of men, who grew beyond their race,
And made themselves as Gods against the fear
Of Death and Hell; and thou that hast from men,
As Queen of Death, that worship which is Fear,
Henceforth, as having risen from out the dead,
Shalt ever send thy life along with mine
From buried grain through springing blade, and bless
Their garnered Autumn also, reap with me,
Earth-mother, in the harvest hymns of Earth
The worship which is Love, and see no more
The Stone, the Wheel, the dimly-glimmering lawns
Of that Elysium, all the hateful fires
Of torment, and the shadowy warrior glide
Along the silent field of Asphodel.

ABOUT POETRY

THE POET'S SONG

The rain had fallen, the Poet arose,
He passed by the town and out of the street,
A light wind blew from the gates of the sun,
And waves of shadow went over the wheat,
And he sat him down in a lonely place,
And chanted a melody loud and sweet,
That made the wild-swan pause in her cloud,
And the lark drop down at his feet.

The swallow stopt as he hunted the bee,
The snake slipt under a spray,
The wild hawk stood with the down on his beak,
And stared, with his foot on the prey,
And the nightingale thought, 'I have sung
many songs,
But never a one so gay,
For he sings of what the world will be
When the years have died away.'

TO VIRGIL

Written at the Request of the Mantuans for the Nineteenth Centenary of Virgil's Death

Roman Virgil, thou that singest
  Ilion's lofty temples robed in fire,
Ilion falling, Rome arising,
  wars, and filial faith, and Dido's pyre;

Landscape-lover, lord of language
  more than he that sang the Works and Days,
All the chosen coin of fancy
  flashing out from many a golden phrase;

Thou that singest wheat and woodland,
  tilth and vineyard, hive and horse and herd;
All the charm of all the Muses
  often flowering in a lonely word;

Poet of the happy Tityrus
  piping underneath his beechen bowers;
Poet of the poet-satyr
  whom the laughing shepherd bound with flowers;

Chanter of the Pollio, glorying
  in the blissful years again to be,
Summers of the snakeless meadow,
  unlaborious earth and oarless sea;

Thou that seëst Universal
 Nature moved by Universal Mind;
Thou majestic in thy sadness
 at the doubtful doom of human kind;

Light among the vanished ages;
 star that gildest yet this phantom shore;
Golden branch amid the shadows,
 kings and realms that pass to rise no more;

Now thy Forum roars no longer,
 fallen every purple Cæsar's dome –
Though thine ocean-roll of rhythm
 sound for ever of Imperial Rome –

Now the Rome of slaves hath perished,
 and the Rome of freemen holds her place,
I, from out the Northern Island
 sundered once from all the human race,

I salute thee, Mantovano,
 I that loved thee since my day began,
Wielder of the stateliest measure
 ever moulded by the lips of man.

WHAT THOR SAID TO THE BARD BEFORE DINNER

Wherever evil customs thicken
Break through with the hammer of iron rhyme,
Till priest-craft and king-craft sicken,
But pap-meat-pamper not the time
With the flock of the thunder-stricken.

If the world caterwaul, lay harder upon her
Till she clapperclaw no longer,
Bang thy stithy stronger and stronger,
Thy rhyme-hammer *shall* have honour.

Be not fairspoken neither stammer,
Nail her, knuckle her, thou swinge-buckler!
Spare not: ribroast gaffer and gammer,
Be no shuffler, wear no muffler,
But on thine anvil hammer and hammer!
If she call out lay harder upon her,
This way and that, nail
Tagrag and bobtail,
Thy rhyme-hammer *shall* have honour.

On squire and parson, broker and banker,
Down let fall thine iron spanker,
Spare not king or duke or critic,

Dealing out cross-buttock and flanker
   With thy clanging analytic!
If she call out lay harder upon her,
   Stun her, stagger her,
   Care not for swaggerer,
Thy rhyme-hammer *shall* have honour.

THE GOLDEN YEAR

Well, you shall have that song which Leonard wrote:
It was last summer on a tour in Wales:
Old James was with me: we that day had been
Up Snowdon; and I wished for Leonard there,
And found him in Llanberis: then we crost
Between the lakes, and clambered half way up
The counter side; and that same song of his
He told me; for I bantered him, and swore
They said he lived shut up within himself,
A tongue-tied Poet in the feverous days,
That, setting the *how much* before the *how*,
Cry, like the daughters of the horseleech, 'Give,
Cram us with all,' but count not me the herd!

   To which 'They call me what they will,' he said:
'But I was born too late: the fair new forms,

That float about the threshold of an age,
Like truths of Science waiting to be caught –
Catch me who can, and make the catcher crowned –
Are taken by the forelock. Let it be.
But if you care indeed to listen, hear
These measured words, my work of yestermorn.

'We sleep and wake and sleep, but all things move;
The Sun flies forward to his brother Sun;
The dark Earth follows wheeled in her ellipse;
And human things returning on themselves
Move onward, leading up the golden year.
'Ah, though the times, when some new thought
can bud,
Are but as poets' seasons when they flower,
Yet seas, that daily gain upon the shore,
Have ebb and flow conditioning their march,
And slow and sure comes up the golden year.
'When wealth no more shall rest in mounded heaps,
But smit with freër light shall slowly melt
In many streams to fatten lower lands,
And light shall spread, and man be liker man
Through all the season of the golden year.
'Shall eagles not be eagles? wrens be wrens?
If all the world were falcons, what of that?
The wonder of the eagle were the less,
But he not less the eagle. Happy days

Roll onward, leading up the golden year.
'Fly, happy happy sails and bear the Press;
Fly happy with the mission of the Cross;
Knit land to land, and blowing havenward
With silks, and fruits, and spices, clear of toll,
Enrich the markets of the golden year.
'But we grow old. Ah! when shall all men's good
Be each man's rule, and universal Peace
Lie like a shaft of light across the land,
And like a lane of beams athwart the sea,
Through all the circle of the golden year?'

Thus far he flowed, and ended; whereupon
'Ah, folly!' in mimic cadence answered James –
'Ah, folly! for it lies so far away,
Not in our time, nor in our children's time,
'Tis like the second world to us that live;
'Twere all as one to fix our hopes on Heaven
As on this vision of the golden year.'

With that he struck his staff against the rocks
And broke it, – James, – you know him, – old, but full
Of force and choler, and firm upon his feet,
And like an oaken stock in winter woods,
O'erflourished with the hoary clematis:
Then added, all in heat:
'What stuff is this!

Old writers pushed the happy season back, –
The more fools they, – we forward: dreamers both:
You most, that in an age, when every hour
Must sweat her sixty minutes to the death
Live on, God love us, as if the seedsman, rapt
Upon the teeming harvest, should not plunge
His hand into the bag: but well I know
That unto him who works, and feels he works,
This same grand year is ever at the doors.'

He spoke; and, high above, I heard them blast
The steep slate-quarry, and the great echo flap
And buffet round the hills from bluff to bluff.

MERLIN AND THE GLEAM

O young Mariner,
You from the haven
Under the sea-cliff,
You that are watching
The grey Magician
With eyes of wonder,
I am Merlin,
And *I* am dying,
I am Merlin
Who follow The Gleam.

Mighty the Wizard
Who found me at sunrise
Sleeping, and woke me
And learned me Magic!
Great the Master,
And sweet the Magic,
When over the valley,
In early summers,
Over the mountain,
On human faces,
And all around me,
Moving to melody,
Floated The Gleam.

Once at the croak of a Raven
who crost it,
A barbarous people,
Blind to the magic,
And deaf to the melody,
Snarled at and cursed me.
A demon vext me,
The light retreated,
The landskip darkened,
The melody deadened,
The Master whispered
'Follow The Gleam.'

Then to the melody,
Over a wilderness
Gliding, and glancing at
Elf of the woodland,
Gnome of the cavern,
Griffin and Giant,
And dancing of Fairies
In desolate hollows,
And wraiths of the mountain,
And rolling of dragons
By warble of water,
Or cataract music
Of falling torrents,
Flitted The Gleam.

Down from the mountain
And over the level,
And streaming and shining on
Silent river,
Silvery willow,
Pasture and plowland,
Innocent maidens,
Garrulous children,
Homestead and harvest,
Reaper and gleaner,
And rough-ruddy faces
Of lowly labour,
Slided The Gleam –

Then, with a melody
Stronger and statelier,
Led me at length
To the city and palace
Of Arthur the king;
Touched at the golden
Cross of the churches,
Flashed on the Tournament,
Flickered and bickered
From helmet to helmet,
And last on the forehead
Of Arthur the blameless
Rested The Gleam.

Clouds and darkness
Closed upon Camelot;
Arthur had vanished
I knew not whither,
The king who loved me,
And cannot die;
For out of the darkness
Silent and slowly
The Gleam, that had waned
to a wintry glimmer
On icy fallow
And faded forest,
Drew to the valley

Named of the shadow,
And slowly brightening
Out of the glimmer,
And slowly moving again to a melody
Yearningly tender,
Fell on the shadow,
No longer a shadow,
But clothed with The Gleam.

And broader and brighter
The Gleam flying onward,
Wed to the melody,
Sang through the world;
And slower and fainter,
Old and weary,
But eager to follow,
I saw, whenever
In passing it glanced upon
Hamlet or city,
That under the Crosses
The dead man's garden,
The mortal hillock,
Would break into blossom;
And so to the land's
Last limit I came –
And can no longer,
But die rejoicing,

For through the Magic
Of Him the Mighty,
Who taught me in childhood,
There on the border
Of boundless Ocean,
And all but in Heaven
Hovers The Gleam.

Not of the sunlight,
Not of the moonlight,
Not of the starlight!
O young Mariner,
Down to the haven,
Call your companions,
Launch your vessel,
And crowd your canvas,
And, ere it vanishes
Over the margin,
After it, follow it,
Follow The Gleam.

PUBLIC VERSE

ENGLAND AND AMERICA IN 1782

O thou, that sendest out the man
  To rule by land and sea,
Strong mother of a Lion-line,
Be proud of those strong sons of thine
  Who wrenched their rights from thee!

What wonder, if in noble heat
  Those men thine arms withstood,
Retaught the lesson thou hadst taught,
And in thy spirit with thee fought –
  Who sprang from English blood!

But Thou rejoice with liberal joy,
  Lift up thy rocky face,
And shatter, when the storms are black,
In many a streaming torrent back,
  The seas that shock thy base!

Whatever harmonies of law
  The growing world assume,
Thy work is thine – The single note
From that deep chord which Hampden smote
  Will vibrate to the doom.

OF OLD SAT FREEDOM ON THE HEIGHTS

Of old sat Freedom on the heights,
The thunders breaking at her feet:
Above her shook the starry lights:
She heard the torrents meet.

There in her place she did rejoice,
Self-gathered in her prophet-mind,
But fragments of her mighty voice
Came rolling on the wind.

Then stept she down through town and field
To mingle with the human race,
And part by part to men revealed
The fullness of her face –

Grave mother of majestic works,
From her isle-altar gazing down,
Who, God-like, grasps the triple forks,
And, King-like, wears the crown:

Her open eyes desire the truth.
The wisdom of a thousand years
Is in them. May perpetual youth
Keep dry their light from tears;

That her fair form may stand and shine,
  Make bright our days and light our dreams,
Turning to scorn with lips divine
  The falsehood of extremes!

LOVE THOU THY LAND, WITH LOVE FAR-BROUGHT

Love thou thy land, with love far-brought
  From out the storied Past, and used
  Within the Present, but transfused
Through future time by power of thought.

True love turned round on fixèd poles,
  Love, that endures not sordid ends,
  For English natures, freemen, friends,
Thy brothers and immortal souls.

But pamper not a hasty time,
  Nor feed with crude imaginings
  The herd, wild hearts and feeble wings,
That every sophister can lime.

Deliver not the tasks of might
 To weakness, neither hide the ray
 From those, not blind, who wait for day,
Though sitting girt with doubtful light.

Make knowledge circle with the winds;
 But let her herald, Reverence, fly
 Before her to whatever sky
Bear seed of men and growth of minds.

Watch what main-currents draw the years:
 Cut Prejudice against the grain:
 But gentle words are always gain:
Regard the weakness of thy peers:

Nor toil for title, place, or touch
 Of pension, neither count on praise:
 It grows to guerdon after-days:
Nor deal in watch-words overmuch;

Not clinging to some ancient saw;
 Not mastered by some modern term;
 Not swift nor slow to change, but firm
And in its season bring the law;

That from Discussion's lip may fall
 With Life, that, working strongly, binds –

Set in all lights by many minds,
To close the interests of all.

For Nature also, cold and warm,
And moist and dry, devising long,
Through many agents making strong,
Matures the individual form.

Meet is it changes should control
Our being, lest we rust in ease.
We all are changed by still degrees
All but the basis of the soul.

So let the change which comes be free
To ingroove itself with that which flies,
And work, a joint of state, that plies
Its office, moved with sympathy.

A saying, hard to shape in act;
For all the past of Time reveals
A bridal dawn of thunder-peals,
Wherever Thought hath wedded Fact.

Ev'n now we hear with inward strife
A motion toiling in the gloom –
The Spirit of the years to come
Yearning to mix himself with Life.

A slow-developed strength awaits
Completion in a painful school;
Phantoms of other forms of rule,
New Majesties of mighty States –

The warders of the growing hour,
But vague in vapour, hard to mark;
And round them sea and air are dark
With great contrivances of Power.

Of many changes, aptly joined,
Is bodied forth the second whole.
Regard gradation, lest the soul
Of Discord race the rising wind;

A wind to puff your idol-fires,
And heap their ashes on the head;
To shame the boast so often made,
That we are wiser than our sires.

Oh yet, if Nature's evil star
Drive men in manhood, as in youth,
To follow flying steps of Truth
Across the brazen bridge of war –

If New and Old, disastrous feud,
Must ever shock, like armèd foes,

And this be true, till Time shall close
That Principles are rained in blood;

Not yet the wise of heart would cease
To hold his hope through shame and guilt,
But with his hand against the hilt,
Would pace the troubled land, like Peace;

Not less, though dogs of Faction bay,
Would serve his kind in deed and word,
Certain, if knowledge bring the sword,
That knowledge takes the sword away –

Would love the gleams of good that broke
From either side, nor veil his eyes
And if some dreadful need should rise
Would strike, and firmly, and one stroke:

To-morrow yet would reap to-day,
As we bear blossom of the dead;
Earn well the thrifty months, nor wed
Raw Haste, half-sister to Delay.

THE CHARGE OF THE LIGHT BRIGADE

Half a league, half a league,
  Half a league onward,
All in the valley of Death
  Rode the six hundred.
'Forward, the Light Brigade!
Charge for the guns!' he said;
Into the valley of Death
  Rode the six hundred.

'Forward, the Light Brigade!'
Was there a man dismayed?
Not though the soldier knew
  Some one had blundered:
Their's not to make reply,
Their's not to reason why,
Their's but to do and die:
Into the valley of Death
  Rode the six hundred.

Cannon to right of them,
Cannon to left of them,
Cannon in front of them
  Volleyed and thundered;
Stormed at with shot and shell,

Boldly they rode and well,
Into the jaws of Death,
Into the mouth of Hell
  Rode the six hundred.

Flashed all their sabres bare,
Flashed as they turned in air,
Sabring the gunners there,
Charging an army, while
  All the world wondered:
Plunged in the battery-smoke
Right through the line they broke;
Cossack and Russian
Reeled from the sabre-stroke
  Shattered and sundered.
Then they rode back, but not,
  Not the six hundred.

Cannon to right of them,
Cannon to left of them,
Cannon behind them
  Volleyed and thundered;
Stormed at with shot and shell,
While horse and hero fell,

They that had fought so well
Came through the jaws of Death
Back from the mouth of Hell,
All that was left of them,
  Left of six hundred.

When can their glory fade?
O the wild charge they made!
  All the world wondered.
Honour the charge they made!
Honour the Light Brigade,
  Noble six hundred!

ODE ON THE DEATH OF THE DUKE OF WELLINGTON

I

Bury the Great Duke
  With an empire's lamentation,
Let us bury the Great Duke
  To the noise of the mourning of a mighty nation,
Mourning when their leaders fall,
Warriors carry the warrior's pall,
And sorrow darkens hamlet and hall.

II

Where shall we lay the man whom we deplore?
Here, in streaming London's central roar.
Let the sound of those he wrought for,
And the feet of those he fought for,
Echo round his bones for evermore.

III

Lead out the pageant: sad and slow,
As fits an universal woe,
Let the long long procession go,
And let the sorrowing crowd about it grow,
And let the mournful martial music blow:
The last great Englishman is low.

IV

Mourn, for to us he seems the last,
Remembering all his greatness in the Past.
No more in soldier fashion will he greet
With lifted hand the gazer in the street.
O friends, our chief state-oracle is mute:
Mourn for the man of long-enduring blood,
The statesman-warrior, moderate, resolute,
Whole in himself, a common good.
Mourn for the man of amplest influence,
Yet clearest of ambitious crime,
Our greatest yet with least pretence,

Great in council and great in war,
Foremost captain of his time,
Rich in saving common-sense,
And, as the greatest only are,
In his simplicity sublime.
O good grey head which all men knew,
O voice from which their omens all men drew,
O iron nerve to true occasion true,
O fallen at length that tower of strength
Which stood four-square to all the winds that blew!
Such was he whom we deplore.
The long self-sacrifice of life is o'er.
The great World-victor's victor will be seen no more.

V

All is over and done:
Render thanks to the Giver,
England, for thy son.
Let the bell be tolled.
Render thanks to the Giver,
And render him to the mould.
Under the cross of gold
That shines over city and river,
There he shall rest for ever
Among the wise and the bold.
Let the bell be tolled:
And a reverent people behold

The towering car, the sable steeds:
Bright let it be with its blazoned deeds,
Dark in its funeral fold.
Let the bell be tolled:
And a deeper knell in the heart be knolled;
And the sound of the sorrowing anthem rolled
Through the dome of the golden cross;
And the volleying cannon thunder his loss;
He knew their voices of old.
For many a time in many a clime
His captain's-ear has heard them boom
Bellowing victory, bellowing doom:
When he with those deep voices wrought,
Guarding realms and kings from shame;
With those deep voices our dead captain taught
The tyrant, and asserts his claim
In that dread sound to the great name,
Which he has worn so pure of blame,
In praise and in dispraise the same,
A man of well-attempered frame.
O civic muse, to such a name,
To such a name for ages long,
To such a name
Preserve a broad approach of fame,
And ever-echoing avenues of song.

VI

Who is he that cometh, like an honoured guest,
With banner and with music, with soldier
and with priest,
With a nation weeping, and breaking on my rest?
Mighty Seaman, this is he
Was great by land as thou by sea.
Thine island loves thee well, thou famous man,
The greatest sailor since our world began.
Now, to the roll of muffled drums,
To thee the greatest soldier comes;
For this is he
Was great by land as thou by sea;
His foes were thine; he kept us free;
O give him welcome, this is he
Worthy of our gorgeous rites,
And worthy to be laid by thee;
For this is England's greatest son,
He that gained a hundred fights,
Nor ever lost an English gun;
This is he that far away
Against the myriads of Assaye
Clashed with his fiery few and won,
And underneath another sun,
Warring on a later day,
Round affrighted Lisbon drew
The treble works, the vast designs

Of his laboured rampart-lines,
Where he greatly stood at bay,
Whence he issued forth anew,
And ever great and greater grew,
Beating from the wasted vines
Back to France her banded swarms,
Back to France with countless blows,
Till o'er the hills her eagles flew
Beyond the Pyrenean pines,
Followed up in valley and glen
With blare of bugle, clamour of men,
Roll of cannon and clash of arms,
And England pouring on her foes.
Such a war had such a close.
Again their ravening eagle rose
In anger, wheeled on Europe-shadowing wings,
And barking for the thrones of kings;
Till one that sought but Duty's iron crown
On that loud sabbath shook the spoiler down;
A day of onsets of despair!
Dashed on every rocky square
Their surging charges foamed themselves away;
Last, the Prussian trumpet blew;
Through the long-tormented air
Heaven flashed a sudden jubilant ray,
And down we swept and charged and overthrew.
So great a soldier taught us there,

What long-enduring hearts could do
In that world's-earthquake, Waterloo!
Mighty Seaman, tender and true,
And pure as he from taint of craven guile,
O saviour of the silver-coasted isle,
O shaker of the Baltic and the Nile,
If aught of things that here befall
Touch a spirit among things divine,
If love of country move thee there at all,
Be glad, because his bones are laid by thine!
And through the centuries let a people's voice
In full acclaim,
A people's voice,
The proof and echo of all human fame,
A people's voice, when they rejoice
At civic revel and pomp and game,
Attest their great commander's claim
With honour, honour, honour, honour to him,
Eternal honour to his name.

VII

A people's voice! we are a people yet.
Though all men else their nobler dreams forget,
Confused by brainless mobs and lawless Powers;
Thank Him who isled us here, and roughly set
His Briton in blown seas and storming showers,
We have a voice, with which to pay the debt

Of boundless love and reverence and regret
To those great men who fought, and kept it ours.
And keep it ours, O God, from brute control;
O Statesmen, guard us, guard the eye, the soul
Of Europe, keep our noble England whole,
And save the one true seed of freedom sown
Betwixt a people and their ancient throne,
That sober freedom out of which there springs
Our loyal passion for our temperate kings;
For, saving that, ye help to save mankind
Till public wrong be crumbled into dust,
And drill the raw world for the march of mind,
Till crowds at length be sane and crowns be just.
But wink no more in slothful overtrust.
Remember him who led your hosts;
He bad you guard the sacred coasts.
Your cannons moulder on the seaward wall:
His voice is silent in your council-hall
For ever; and whatever tempests lour
For ever silent; even if they broke
In thunder, silent; yet remember all
He spoke among you, and the Man who spoke;
Who never sold the truth to serve the hour,
Nor paltered with Eternal God for power;
Who let the turbid streams of rumour flow
Through either babbling world of high and low;
Whose life was work, whose language rife

With rugged maxims hewn from life;
Who never spoke against a foe;
Whose eighty winters freeze with one rebuke
All great self-seekers trampling on the right:
Truth-teller was our England's Alfred named;
Truth-lover was our English Duke;
Whatever record leap to light
He never shall be shamed.

VIII

Lo, the leader in these glorious wars
Now to glorious burial slowly borne,
Followed by the brave of other lands,
He, on whom from both her open hands
Lavish Honour showered all her stars,
And affluent Fortune emptied all her horn.
Yea, let all good things await
Him who cares not to be great,
But as he saves or serves the state.
Not once or twice in our rough island-story,
The path of duty was the way to glory;
He that walks it, only thirsting
For the right, and learns to deaden
Love of self, before his journey closes,
He shall find the stubborn thistle bursting
Into glossy purples, which outredden
All voluptuous garden-roses.

Not once or twice in our fair island-story,
The path of duty was the way to glory:
He, that ever following her commands,
On with toil of heart and knees and hands,
Through the long gorge to the far light has won
His path upward, and prevailed,
Shall find the toppling crags of Duty scaled
Are close upon the shining table-lands
To which our God Himself is moon and sun.
Such was he: his work is done,
But while the races of mankind endure,
Let his great example stand
Colossal, seen of every land,
And keep the soldier firm, the statesman pure:
Till in all lands and through all human story
The path of duty be the way to glory:
And let the land whose hearths he saved from shame
For many and many an age proclaim
At civic revel and pomp and game,
And when the long-illumined cities flame,
Their ever-loyal iron leader's fame,
With honour, honour, honour, honour to him,
Eternal honour to his name.

IX

Peace, his triumph will be sung
By some yet unmoulded tongue

Far on in summers that we shall not see:
Peace, it is a day of pain
For one about whose patriarchal knee
Late the little children clung:
O peace, it is a day of pain
For one, upon whose hand and heart and brain
Once the weight and fate of Europe hung.
Ours the pain, be his the gain!
More than is of man's degree
Must be with us, watching here
At this, our great solemnity.
Whom we see not we revere,
We revere, and we refrain
From talk of battles loud and vain,
And brawling memories all too free
For such a wise humility
As befits a solemn fane:
We revere, and while we hear
The tides of Music's golden sea
Setting toward eternity,
Uplifted high in heart and hope are we,
Until we doubt not that for one so true
There must be other nobler work to do
Than when he fought at Waterloo,
And Victor he must ever be.
For though the Giant Ages heave the hill
And break the shore, and evermore

Make and break, and work their will;
Though world on world in myriad myriads roll
Round us, each with different powers,
And other forms of life than ours,
What know we greater than the soul?
On God and Godlike men we build our trust.
Hush, the Dead March wails in the people's ears:
The dark crowd moves, and there are sobs and tears:
The black earth yawns: the mortal disappears;
Ashes to ashes, dust to dust;
He is gone who seemed so great. –
Gone; but nothing can bereave him
Of the force he made his own
Being here, and we believe him
Something far advanced in State,
And that he wears a truer crown
Than any wreath that man can weave him.
Speak no more of his renown,
Lay your earthly fancies down,
And in the vast cathedral leave him.
God accept him, Christ receive him.

FRAGMENTS AND EXPERIMENTS

EPIGRAMS

CIRCUMSTANCE

Two children in two neighbour villages
Playing mad pranks along the heathy leas;
Two strangers meeting at a festival
Two lovers whispering by an orchard wall;
Two lives bound fast in one with golden ease;
Two graves grass-green beside a grey church-tower,
Washed with still rains and daisy-blossomed;
Two children in one hamlet born and bred;
So runs the round of life from hour to hour.

WE ARE FREE

The winds, as at their hour of birth,
  Leaning upon the ridgèd sea,
Breathed low around the rolling earth
  With mellow preludes, 'We are free.'

The streams through many a lilied row
  Down-carolling to the crispèd sea,
Low-tinkled with a bell-like flow
  Atween the blossoms, 'We are free.'

ON ONE WHO AFFECTED AN EFFEMINATE MANNER

While man and woman still are incomplete,
I prize that soul where man and woman meet,
Which types all Nature's male and female plan,
But, friend, man-woman is not woman-man.

TO ONE WHO RAN DOWN THE ENGLISH

You make our faults too gross, and thence maintain
Our darker future. May your fears be vain!
At times the small black fly upon the pane
May seem the black ox of the distant plain.

A QUOTABLE SNATCH OF OVIDIAN SONG

A quotable snatch of Ovidian song
 And a saying true to the letter,
Yet – if we follow the worse too long
 We may cease to believe in the Better.

TRANSLATIONS

BATTLE OF BRUNANBURH

I

Athelstan King,
Lord among Earls,
Bracelet-bestower and
Baron of Barons,
He with his brother,
Edmund Atheling,
Gaining a lifelong
Glory in battle,
Slew with the sword-edge
There by Brunanburh,
Brake the shield-wall,
Hewed the lindenwood,
Hacked the battleshield,
Sons of Edward with hammered brands.

II

Theirs was a greatness
Got from their Grandsires –
Theirs that so often in
Strife with their enemies
Struck for their hoards and their hearths and
their homes.

III

Bowed the spoiler,
Bent the Scotsman,
Fell the shipcrews
Doomed to the death.
All the field with blood of the fighters
Flowed, from when first the great
Sun-star of morningtide,
Lamp of the Lord God
Lord everlasting,
Glode over earth till the glorious creature
Sank to his setting.

IV

There lay many a man
Marred by the javelin,
Men of the Northland
Shot over shield.
There was the Scotsman
Weary of war.

V

We the West-Saxons,
Long as the daylight
Lasted, in companies
Troubled the track of the host that we hated,
Grimly with swords that were sharp from
the grindstone,
Fiercely we hacked at the flyers before us.

VI

Mighty the Mercian,
Hard was his hand-play,
Sparing not any of
Those that with Anlaf,
Warriors over the
Weltering waters
Borne in the bark's-bosom,
Drew to this island:
Doomed to the death.

VII

Five young kings put asleep by the sword-stroke,
Seven strong Earls of the army of Anlaf
Fell on the war-field, numberless numbers,
Shipmen and Scotsmen.

VIII

Then the Norse leader,
Dire was his need of it,
Few were his following,
Fled to his warship:
Fleeted his vessel to sea with the king in it,
Saving his life on the fallow flood.

IX

Also the crafty one,
Constantinus,
Crept to his North again,
Hoar-headed hero!

X

Slender warrant had
He to be proud of
The welcome of war-knives –
He that was reft of his
Folk and his friends that had
Fallen in conflict,
Leaving his son too
Lost in the carnage,
Mangled to morsels,
A youngster in war!

XI

Slender reason had
He to be glad of
The clash of the war-glaive –
Traitor and trickster
And spurner of treaties –
He nor had Anlaf
With armies so broken
A reason for bragging
That they had the better
In perils of battle
On places of slaughter –
The struggle of standards,
The rush of the javelins,
The crash of the charges,
The wielding of weapons –
The play that they played with
The children of Edward.

XII

Then with their nailed prows
Parted the Norsemen, a
Blood-reddened relic of
Javelins over
The jarring breaker, the deep-sea billow,
Shaping their way toward Dyflen again,
Shamed in their souls.

XIII

Also the brethren,
King and Atheling,
Each in his glory,
Went to his own in his own West-Saxonland,
Glad of the war.

XIV

Many a carcase they left to be carrion,
Many a livid one, many a sallow-skin –
Left for the white tailed eagle to tear it, and
Left for the horny-nibbed raven to rend it, and
Gave to the garbaging war-hawk to gorge it, and
That grey beast, the wolf of the weald.

XV

Never had huger
Slaughter of heroes
Slain by the sword-edge –
Such as old writers
Have writ of in histories –
Hapt in this isle, since
Up from the East hither
Saxon and Angle from
Over the broad billow
Broke into Britain with
Haughty war-workers who

Harried the Welshman, when
Earls that were lured by the
Hunger of glory gat
Hold of the land.

SPECIMEN OF A TRANSLATION OF THE *ILIAD* IN BLANK VERSE

So Hector said, and sea-like roared his host;
Then loosed their sweating horses from the yoke,
And each beside his chariot bound his own;
And oxen from the city, and goodly sheep
In haste they drove, and honey-hearted wine
And bread from out the houses brought, and heaped
Their firewood, and the winds from off the plain
Rolled the rich vapour far into the heaven.
And these all night upon the bridge of war
Sat glorying; many a fire before them blazed:
As when in heaven the stars about the moon
Look beautiful, when all the winds are laid,
And every height comes out, and jutting peak
And valley, and the immeasurable heavens
Break open to their highest, and all the stars
Shine, and the Shepherd gladdens in his heart:
So many a fire between the ships and stream

Of Xanthus blazed before the towers of Troy
A thousand on the plain; and close by each
Sat fifty in the blaze of burning fire;
And champing golden grain, their horses stood
Hard by the chariots, waiting for the dawn.

METRICAL EXPERIMENTS

SEMELE: A FRAGMENT

I wished to see Him. Who may feel
His light and live? He comes.
The blast of Godhead bursts the doors,
His mighty hands are twined
About the triple forks, and when He speaks
The crown of sunlight shudders round
Ambrosial temples, and aloft,
Fluttering through Elysian air,
His green and azure mantles float in wavy
Foldings, and melodious thunder
Wheels in circles.
But thou, my son, who shalt be born
When I am ashes, to delight the world –

Now with measured cymbal-clash
Moving on to victory;
Now on music-rolling orbs,
A sliding throne, voluptuously
Panther-drawn,
To throbbings of the thunderous gong,
And melody o' the merrily-blowing flute;
Now with troops of clamorous revellers,
Merrily, merrily,
Rapidly, giddily,
Rioting, triumphing
Bacchanalians,
Rushing in cadence,
All in order,
Plunging down the viney valleys –

MILTON

Alcaics

O mighty-mouthed inventor of harmonies,
O skilled to sing of Time or Eternity,
    God-gifted organ-voice of England,
        Milton, a name to resound for ages;
Whose Titan angels, Gabriel, Abdiel,
Starred from Jehovah's gorgeous armouries,

Tower, as the deep-domed empyrëan
Rings to the roar of an angel onset –
Me rather all that bowery loneliness,
The brooks of Eden mazily murmuring,
And bloom profuse and cedar arches
Charm, as a wanderer out in ocean,
Where some refulgent sunset of India
Streams o'er a rich ambrosial ocean isle
And crimson-hued the stately palmwoods
Whisper in odorous heights of even.

Hendecasyllabics

O you chorus of indolent reviewers,
Irresponsible, indolent reviewers,
Look, I come to the test, a tiny poem
All composed in a metre of Catullus,
All in quantity, careful of my motion,
Like the skater on ice that hardly bears him,
Lest I fall unawares before the people,
Waking laughter in indolent reviewers.
Should I flounder awhile without a tumble
Through this metrification of Catullus,
They should speak to me not without a welcome,
All that chorus of indolent reviewers.

Hard, hard, hard is it, only not to tumble,
So fantastical is the dainty metre.
Wherefore slight me not wholly, nor believe me
Too presumptuous, indolent reviewers.
O blatant Magazines, regard me rather –
Since I blush to belaud myself a moment –
As some rare little rose, a piece of inmost
Horticultural art, or half coquette-like
Maiden, not to be greeted unbenignly.

ON TRANSLATIONS OF HOMER

Hexameters and Pentameters

These lame hexameters the strong-winged music
of Homer!
No – but a most burlesque barbarous experiment.
When was a harsher sound ever heard, ye Muses,
in England?
When did a frog coarser croak upon our Helicon?
Hexameters no worse than daring Germany gave us,
Barbarous experiment, barbarous hexameters!

ILION, ILION

Ilion, Ilion, dreamy Ilion, pillared Ilion, holy Ilion,
City of Ilion when wilt thou be melody born?
Blue Scamander, yellowing Simois from the heart
        of piny Ida
Everwhirling from the molten snows upon
        the mountainthrone,
Roll Scamander, ripple Simois, ever onward to a melody
Manycircled, overflowing thorough and thorough the
        flowery level of unbuilt Ilion,
City of Ilion, pillared Ilion, shadowy Ilion, holy Ilion,
    To a music merrily flowing, merrily echoing
    When wilt thou be melody born?

Manygated, heavywallèd, manytowered city of Ilion,
From the silver, lilyflowering meadowlevel
    When wilt thou be melody born?
Ripple onward, echoing Simois,
Ripple ever with a melancholy moaning,
    In the rushes to the dark blue brimmèd Ocean,
        yellowing Simois,
To a music from the golden twanging harpwire
        heavily drawn
    Manygated, heavywallèd, manytowered city of Ilion,
    To a music sadly flowing, slowly falling,
    When wilt thou be melody born?

DIALECT POEMS

NORTHERN FARMER

Old Style

Wheer 'asta beän saw long and meä liggin' 'ere aloän?
Noorse? thourt nowt o' a noorse: whoy, Doctor's abeän
 an' agoän:
Says that I moänt 'a naw moor yaäle: but I beänt a fool:
Git ma my yaäle, for I beänt a-gooin' to breäk my rule.

Doctors, they knaws nowt, for a says what's
 nawways true:
Naw soort o' koind o' use to saäy the things that a do.
I've 'ed my point o' yaäle ivry noight sin' I bean 'ere,
An' I've 'ed my quart ivry market-noight for foorty year.

Parson's a beän loikewoise, an' a sittin' 'ere o' my bed.
'The amoighty's a taäkin o' you to 'issén, my friend,'
 a said,

An' a towd ma my sins, an's toithe were due, an' I gied
    it in hond;
I done my duty by un, as I 'a done by the lond.

Larned a ma' beä. I reckons I 'annot sa mooch to larn.
But a cost oop, thot a did, 'boot Bessy Marris's barn.
Thof a knaws I hallus voäted wi' Squoire an' choorch
    an' staäte,
An' i' the woost o' toimes I wur niver agin the raäte.

An' I hallus comed to 's choorch afoor moy Sally
    wur deäd,
An' 'eerd un a bummin' awaäy loike a buzzard-clock
    ower my yeäd,
An' I niver knawed whot a meäned but I thowt a 'ad
    summut to saäy,
An I thowt a said whot a owt to 'a said an' I comed
    awaäy.

Bessy Marris's barn! tha knaws she laäid it to meä.
Mowt 'a beän, mayhap, for she wur a bad un, sheä.
'Siver, I kep un, I kep un, my lass, tha mun understond;
I done my duty by un as I 'a done by the lond.

But Parson a comes an' a goos, an' a says it eäsy an' freeä
'The amoighty's a taäkin' o' you to 'issén, my friend,'
    says 'eä.

I weänt saäy men be loiars, thof summun said it in 'äaste:
But a reäds wonn sarmin a weeäk, an' I 'a stubbed
Thornaby waäste.

D'ya moind the waäste, my lass? naw, naw, tha was not
born then;
Theer wur a boggle in it, I often 'eerd un mysen;
Moäst loike a butter-bump, for I 'eerd un aboot
an' aboot,
But I stubbed un oop wi' the lot, an' raäved an' rembled
un oot.

Keäper's it wur; fo' they fun un theer a-laäid on 'is faäce
Doon i' the woild 'enemies afoor I comed to the plaäce.
Noäks or Thimbleby – toner'ed shot un as deäd
as a naäil.
Noäks wur 'anged for it oop at 'soize – but git ma
my yaäle.

Dubbut looäk at the waäste: theer warn't not feäd
for a cow:
Nowt at all but bracken an' fuzz, an' looäk at it now –
Warnt worth nowt a haäcre, an' now theer's lots o' feäd,
Fourscore yows upon it an' some on it doon in seäd.

Nobbut a bit on it's left, an' I meäned to 'a stubbed it
at fall,

Done it ta-year I meäned, an' runned plow thruff
it an' all,
If godamoighty an' parson 'ud nobbut let ma aloän.
Meä, wi' haäte oonderd haäcre o' Squoire's, an' lond o'
my oän.

Do godamoighty knaw what a's doing a-taäkin'
o' meä?
I beänt wonn as saws 'ere a beän an' yonder a peä;
An' Squoire 'ull be sa mad an' all – a' dear a' dear!
And I 'a monaged for Squoire come Michaelmas
thirty year.

A mowt 'a taäken Joänes, as 'ant 'aäpoth o' sense,
Or a mowt 'a taäken Robins – a niver mended a fence:
But godamoighty a moost taäke meä an' taäke ma now
Wi 'auf the cows to cauve an' Thornaby holms to plow!

Looäk 'ow quoloty smoiles when they sees ma
a passin' by,
Says to thessén naw doot, 'what a mon a beä sewer-ly!'
For they knaws what I beän to Squoire sin fust a comed
to the 'All;
I done my duty by Squoire an' I done my duty by all.

Squoire's in Lunnon, an' summun I reckons 'ull 'a
to wroite,

For who's to howd the lond ater meä thot muddles
ma quoit;
Sartin-sewer I beä, thot a weänt niver give it to Joänes,
Noither a moänt to Robins – a niver rembles the
stoäns.

But summun 'ull come ater meä mayhap wi' 'is kittle
o' steam
Huzzin' an' maäzin' the blessed feälds wi' the Divil's
oän teäm.
Gin I mun doy I mun doy, an' loife they says is sweet,
But gin I mun doy I mun doy, for I couldn abear to
see it.

What atta stannin' theer for, an' doesn bring ma the
yaäle?
Doctor's a 'tottler, lass, an a 's hallus i' the owd taäle;
I weänt breäk rules for Doctor, a knaws naw moor nor
a floy;
Git ma my yaäle I tell tha, an' gin I mun doy I mun doy.

OWD ROÄ

Naäy, noä mander o' use to be callin' 'im Roä, Roä, Roä,
Fur the dog's stoän-deäf, an' 'e's blind, 'e can naither
stan' nor goä.

But I meäns fur to maäke 'is owd aäge as 'appy as iver
I can,
Fur I owäs owd Roäver moor nor I iver owäd mottal
man.

Thou's rode of 'is back when a babby, afoor thou was
gotten too owd,
Fur 'e'd fetch an' carry like owt, 'e was allus as good
as gowd.

Eh, but 'e'd fight wi' a will *when* 'e fowt; 'e could howd
'is oan,
An' Roä was the dog as knawed when an' wheere to bury
his boane.

An' 'e kep his heäd hoop like a king, an' 'e'd niver not
down wi' is taäil,
Fur 'e'd niver done nowt to be shaämed on, when we was
i' Howlaby Daäle.

An' 'e sarved me sa well when 'e lived, that, Dick, when
'e cooms to be deäd,
I thinks as I'd like fur to hev soom soort of a sarvice
reäd.

Fur 'e's moor good sense na the Parliament man 'at stans
fur us 'ere,
An' I'd voät fur 'im, my oän sen, if 'e could but stan fur
the Shere.

'Faäithful an' True' – them words be i' Scriptur – an'
Faäithful an' True
Ull be fun' upo' four short legs ten times fur one
upo' two.

An' maäybe they'll walk upo' two but I knaws they runs
upo' four, –
Bedtime, Dicky! but waäit till tha 'eärs it be strikin'
the hour.

Fur I wants to tell tha o' Roä when we lived i' Howlaby
Daäle,
Ten year sin – Naäy – naäy! tha mun nobbut hev' one
glass of aäle.

Straänge an' owd-farraned the 'ouse, an' belt long afoor
my daäy

Wi' haäfe o' the chimleys a-twizzened an' twined like a
band o' haäy.

The fellers as maäkes them picturs, 'ud coom at the fall
o' the year,
An' sattle their ends upo' stools to pictur the door-
poorch theere,

An' the Heagle 'as hed two heäds stannin' theere o' the
brokken stick;
An' they niver 'ed seed sich ivin' as grawed hall ower
the brick;

An' theere i' the 'ouse one night – but it's down, an' all
on it now
Goan into mangles an' tonups, an' raäved slick thruf by
the plow –

Theere, when the 'ouse wur a house, one night I wur
sittin' aloän,
Wi' Roäver athurt my feeät, an' sleeäpin still as a stoän,

Of a Christmas Eäve, an' as cowd as this, an' the midders
as white,
An' the fences all on 'em bolstered oop wi' the windle
that night;

An' the cat wur a-sleeäpin' alongside Roäver, but I
wur awaäke,
An' smoäkin' an' thinkin' o' things – Doänt maäke
thysen sick wi' the caäke.

Fur the men ater supper 'ed sung their songs an' 'ed 'ed
their beer,
An' 'ed goan their waäys; ther was nobbut three, an'
noän on 'em theere.

They was all on 'em feared o' the Ghoäst an' dussn't not
sleeäp i' the 'ouse,
But Dicky, the Ghoäst moästlins was nobbut a rat
or a mouse.

An' I looökt out wonst at the night, an' the daäle was all
of a thaw,
Fur I seed the beck coomin' down like a long black
snaäke i' the snaw,

An' I heärd great heäps o' the snaw slushin' down fro'
the bank to the beck,
An' then as I stood i' the doorwaäy, I feeäld it drip
o' my neck.

Saw I turned in ageän, an' I thowt o' the good owd times
'at was goan,

An' the munney they maäde by the war, an' the times 'at
was coomin' on;

Fur I thowt if the Staäte was a gawin' to let in furriners'
wheät,
Howiver was British farmers to stan' ageän o' their feeät.

Howiver was I fur to find my rent an' to paäy
my men?
An' all along o' the feller as turned 'is back of hissen.

Thou slep i' the chaumber above us, we couldn't ha' 'eärd
tha call,
Sa Moother 'ed telled ma to bring tha down, an' thy
craädle an' all;

Fur the gell o' the farm 'at slep wi' tha then 'ed gotten
wer leäve,
Fur to goä that night to 'er foälk by cause o' the
Christmas Eäve;

But I cleän forgot tha, my lad, when Moother 'ed gotten
to bed,
An' I slep i' my chair hup-on-end, an' the Freeä Traäde
runned 'i my 'ead,

Till I dreämed 'at Squire walkt in, an' I says to him
'Squire, ya're laäte,'
Then I seed at 'is faäce wur as red as the Yule-block
theer i' the graäte.

An' 'e says 'can ya paäy me the rent tonight?' an' I says
to 'im 'Noä,'
An' 'e cotched howd hard o' my hairm, 'Then hout
tonight tha shall goä.'

'Tha'll niver,' says I, 'be a-turnin' ma hout upo'
Christmas Eäve?'
Then I waäked an' I fun it was Roäver a-tuggin' an'
tearin' my slieäve.

An' I thowt as 'e'd goän cleän-wud, fur I noäwaäys
knawed 'is intent;
An' I says 'Git awaäy, ya beäst,' an' I fetcht 'im a kick an'
'e went.

Then 'e tummled up stairs, fur I 'eard 'im, as if 'e'd 'a
brokken 'is neck,
An' I'd cleär forgot, little Dicky, thy chaumber door
wouldn't sneck;

An' I slep i' my chair ageän wi' my hairm hingin' down
to the floor,

An' I thowt it was Roäver a-tuggin' an' teärin' me wuss
nor afoor.

An' I thowt 'at I kicked 'im ageän, but I kicked thy
Moother istead.
'What arta snorin' theere fur? the house is afire,'
she said.

Thy Moother 'ed beän a-naggin' about the gell
o' the farm,
She offens 'ud spy summut wrong when there warn't not
a mossel o' harm;

An' she didn't not solidly meän I wur gawin' that waäy
to the bad,
Fur the gell was as howry a trollope as iver traäpesed
i' the squad.

But Moother was free of 'er tongue, as I offens 'ev telled
'er mysen,
Sa I kep i' my chair, fur I thowt she was nobbut a-rilin'
ma then.

An' I says 'I'd be good to tha, Bess, if tha'd onywaäys let
ma be good,'
But she skelpt ma haäfe ower i' the chair, an' screeäd like
a Howl gone wud –

'Ya mun run fur the lether. Git oop, if ya're onywaäys
good for owt.'
And I says 'If I beänt noäwaäys – not nowadaäys – good
fur nowt –

Yit I beänt sich a Nowt of all Nowts as 'ull hallus do as
'e's bid.'
'But the stairs is afire,' she said; then I seed 'er a-cryin',
I did.

An' she beäld 'Ya mun saäve little Dick, an' be sharp
about it an' all,'
Sa I runs to the yard fur a lether, an' sets 'im ageän
the wall,

An' I claums an' I mashes the winder hin, when I gits to
the top,
But the heät druv hout i' my heyes till I feäld mysen
ready to drop.

Thy Moother was howdin' the lether, an' tellin' me not
to be skeärd,
An' I wasn't afeärd, or I thinks leästwaäys as I wasn't
afeärd;

But I couldn't see fur the smoäke wheere thou was
a-liggin', my lad,

An' Roäver was theere i' the chaumber a-yowlin' an' yaupin' like mad;

An' thou was a-beälin' likewise, an' a-squeälin', as if tha was bit,
An' it wasn't a bite but a burn, fur the merk's o' thy shou'der yit;

Then I called out Roä, Roä, Roä, thaw I didn't haäfe think as 'e'd 'ear,
But 'e coomed thruf the fire wi' my bairn i' 'is mouth to the winder theere!

He coomed like a Hangel o' marcy as soon as 'e 'eärd 'is naäme,
Or like tother Hangel i' Scriptur 'at summun seed i' the flaäme,

When summun 'ed haxed fur a son, an' 'e promised a son to she,
An' Roä was as good as the Hangel i' saävin' a son fur me.

Sa I browt tha down, an' I says 'I mun gaw up ageän fur Roä.'
'Gaw up ageän fur the varmint?' I telled 'er 'Yeäs I mun goä.'

An' I claumbed up ageän to the winder, an' clemmed owd
Roä by the 'eäd,
An 'is 'air coomed off i' my 'ands an' I taäked 'im at fust
fur deäd;

Fur 'e smelled like a herse a-singein', an' seeämed as
blind as a poop,
An' haäfe on 'im bare as a bublin'. I cauldn't wakken
'im oop,

But I browt 'im down, an' we got to the barn, fur the
barn wouldn't burn
Wi' the wind blawin' hard tother waäy, an' the wind
wasn't like to turn.

An' *I* kep a-callin' o' Roä till 'e waggled 'is taäil fur
a bit,
But the cocks kep a-crawin' an' crawin' all night, an'
I 'ears 'em yit;

An' the dogs was a-yowlin' all round, and thou was
a-squeälin' thysen,
An' Moother was naggin' an' groänin' an' moänin' an'
naggin' ageän;

An' I 'eärd the bricks an' the baulks rummle down when
the roof gev waäy,

Fur the fire was a-raägin' an' raävin' an' roarin' like
judgment daäy.

Warm enew theere sewer-ly, but the barn was as cowd
as owt,
An' we cuddled and huddled togither, an' happt wersens
oop as we mowt.

An' I browt Roä round, but Moother 'ed beän sa soäked
wi' the thaw
'At she cotched 'er death o' cowd that night, poor soul,
i' the straw.

Haäfe o' the parish runned oop when the rigtree was
tummlin' in –
Too laäte – but it's all ower now – hall hower – an' ten
year sin;

Too laäte, tha mun git tha to bed, but I'll coom an' I'll
squench the light,
Fur we moänt 'ev naw moor fires – and soa little Dick,
good-night.

IN MEMORIAM

ON A MOURNER

Nature, so far as in her lies,
  Imitates God, and turns her face
To every land beneath the skies,
  Counts nothing that she meets with base,
  But lives and loves in every place;

Fills out the homely quickset-screens,
  And makes the purple lilac ripe,
Steps from her airy hill, and greens
  The swamp, where hums the dropping snipe,
  With moss and braided marish-pipe;

And on thy heart a finger lays,
  Saying, 'Beat quicker, for the time
Is pleasant, and the woods and ways
  Are pleasant, and the beech and lime
  Put forth and feel a gladder clime.'

And murmurs of a deeper voice,
  Going before to some far shrine,
Teach that sick heart the stronger choice,
  Till all thy life one way incline
  With one wide will that closes thine.

And when the zoning eve has died
Where yon dark valleys wind forlorn,
Come Hope and Memory, spouse and bride,
From out the borders of the morn,
With that fair child betwixt them born.

And when no mortal motion jars
The blackness round the tombing sod,
Through silence and the trembling stars
Comes Faith from tracts no feet have trod,
And Virtue, like a household god

Promising empire; such as those
That once at dead of night did greet
Troy's wandering prince, so that he rose
With sacrifice, while all the fleet
Had rest by stony hills of Crete.

THE ANTE-CHAMBER

That is his portrait painted by himself.
Look on those manly curls so glossy dark,
Those thoughtful furrows in the swarthy cheek;
Admire that stalwart shape, those ample brows,
And that large table of the breast dispread,
Between low shoulders; how demure a smile,
How full of wisest humour and of love,
With some half-consciousness of inward power,
Sleeps round those quiet lips; not quite a smile;
And look you what an arch the brain has built
Above the ear! and what a settled mind,
Mature, harboured from change, contemplative,
Tempers the peaceful light of hazel eyes,
Observing all things. This is he I loved,
This is the man of whom you heard me speak.
  My fancy was the more luxurious,
But his was minted in a deeper mould,
And took in more of Nature than mine own:
Nor proved I such delight as he, to mark
The humours of the polling and the wake,
The hubbub of the market and the booths:
How this one smiled, that other waved his arms,
These careful and those candid brows, how each –
Down to his slightest turns and attitudes –
Was something that another could not be,

How every brake and flower spread and rose,
Distinct in individualities,
A various world! which he compelled once more
Through his own nature, with well mingled hues,
Into another shape, born of the first,
As beautiful, but yet another world.
  All this so stirred him in his hour of joy,
Mixed with the phantom of his coming fame,
That once he spake: 'I lift the eyes of thought,
I look through all my glimmering life, I see
At the end, as 'twere athwart a coloured cloud,
O'er the bowed shoulder of a bland old Age,
The face of placid Death.' Long, Eustace, long
May my strong wish, transgressing the low bound
Of mortal hope, act on Eternity
To keep thee here amongst us! Yet he lives;
His and my friendship have not suffered loss,
His fame is equal to his years: his praise
Is neither overdealt, nor idly won.
  Step through these doors, and I will show to you
Another countenance, one yet more dear,
More dear, for what is lost is made more dear;
'More dear' I will not say, but rather bless
The All-perfect Framer, Him, who made the heart,
Forethinking its twinfold necessity,
Through one whole life an overflowing urn,
Capacious both of Friendship and of Love.

From IN MEMORIAM A. H. H.

OBIIT MDCCCXXXIII

Strong Son of God, immortal Love,
  Whom we, that have not seen thy face,
  By faith, and faith alone, embrace,
Believing where we cannot prove;

Thine are these orbs of light and shade;
  Thou madest Life in man and brute;
  Thou madest Death; and lo, thy foot
Is on the skull which thou hast made.

Thou wilt not leave us in the dust:
  Thou madest man, he knows not why;
  He thinks he was not made to die;
And thou hast made him: thou art just.

Thou seemest human and divine,
  The highest, holiest manhood, thou:
  Our wills are ours, we know not how;
Our wills are ours, to make them thine.

Our little systems have their day;
  They have their day and cease to be:
  They are but broken lights of thee,
And thou, O Lord, art more than they.

We have but faith: we cannot know;
  For knowledge is of things we see;
  And yet we trust it comes from thee,
A beam in darkness: let it grow.

Let knowledge grow from more to more,
  But more of reverence in us dwell;
  That mind and soul, according well,
May make one music as before,

But vaster. We are fools and slight;
  We mock thee when we do not fear:
  But help thy foolish ones to bear;
Help thy vain worlds to bear thy light.

Forgive what seemed my sin in me;
  What seemed my worth since I began;
  For merit lives from man to man,
And not from man, O Lord, to thee.

Forgive my grief for one removed,
  Thy creature, whom I found so fair.
  I trust he lives in thee, and there
I find him worthier to be loved.

Forgive these wild and wandering cries,
  Confusions of a wasted youth;

Forgive them where they fail in truth,
And ill thy wisdom make me wise.

I

I held it truth, with him who sings
To one clear harp in divers tones,
That men may rise on stepping-stones
Of their dead selves to higher things.

But who shall so forecast the years
And find in loss a gain to match?
Or reach a hand through time to catch
The far-off interest of tears?

Let Love clasp Grief lest both be drowned,
Let darkness keep her raven gloss:
Ah, sweeter to be drunk with loss,
To dance with death, to beat the ground,

Than that the victor Hours should scorn
The long result of love, and boast,
'Behold the man that loved and lost,
But all he was is overworn.'

II

Old Yew, which graspest at the stones
That name the under-lying dead,

Thy fibres net the dreamless head,
Thy roofs are wrapt about the bones.

The seasons bring the flower again,
And bring the firstling to the flock;
And in the dusk of thee, the clock
Beats out the little lives of men.

O not for thee the glow, the bloom,
Who changest not in any gale,
Nor branding summer suns avail
To touch thy thousand years of gloom:

And gazing on thee, sullen tree,
Sick for thy stubborn hardihood,
I seem to fail from out my blood
And grow incorporate into thee.

III

O Sorrow, cruel fellowship,
O Priestess in the vaults of Death,
O sweet and bitter in a breath,
What whispers from thy lying lip?

'The stars,' she whispers, 'blindly run;
A web is wov'n across the sky;
From out waste places comes a cry,
And murmurs from the dying sun:

'And all the phantom, Nature, stands –
With all the music in her tone,
A hollow echo of my own, –
A hollow form with empty hands.'

And shall I take a thing so blind,
Embrace her as my natural good;
Or crush her, like a vice of blood,
Upon the threshold of the mind?

IV

To Sleep I give my powers away;
My will is bondsman to the dark;
I sit within a helmless bark,
And with my heart I muse and say:

O heart, how fares it with thee now,
That thou should'st fail from thy desire,
Who scarcely darest to inquire,
'What is it makes me beat so low?'

Something it is which thou hast lost,
Some pleasure from thine early years.
Break, thou deep vase of chilling tears,
That grief hath shaken into frost!

Such clouds of nameless trouble cross
All night below the darkened eyes;

With morning wakes the will, and cries,
'Thou shalt not be the fool of loss.'

V

I sometimes hold it half a sin
To put in words the grief I feel;
For words, like Nature, half reveal
And half conceal the Soul within.

But, for the unquiet heart and brain,
A use in measured language lies;
The sad mechanic exercise,
Like dull narcotics, numbing pain.

In words, like weeds, I'll wrap me o'er,
Like coarsest clothes against the cold;
But that large grief which these enfold
Is given in outline and no more.

VI

One writes, that 'Other friends remain,'
That 'Loss is common to the race' –
And common is the commonplace,
And vacant chaff well meant for grain.

That loss is common would not make
My own less bitter, rather more:

Too common! Never morning wore
To evening, but some heart did break.

O father, wheresoe'er thou be,
Who pledgest now thy gallant son;
A shot, ere half thy draught be done,
Hath stilled the life that beat from thee.

O mother, praying God will save
Thy sailor, – while thy head is bowed,
His heavy-shotted hammock-shroud
Drops in his vast and wandering grave.

Ye know no more than I who wrought
At that last hour to please him well;
Who mused on all I had to tell,
And something written, something thought;

Expecting still his advent home;
And ever met him on his way
With wishes, thinking, 'here to-day,'
Or 'here to-morrow will he come.'

O somewhere, meek unconscious dove,
That sittest ranging golden hair,
And glad to find thyself so fair,
Poor child, that waitest for thy love!

For now her father's chimney glows
  In expectation of a guest;
  And thinking 'this will please him best,'
She takes a riband or a rose;

For he will see them on to-night;
  And with the thought her colour burns;
  And, having left the glass, she turns
Once more to set a ringlet right;

And, even when she turned, the curse
  Had fallen, and her future Lord
  Was drowned in passing through the ford,
Or killed in falling from his horse.

O what to her shall be the end?
  And what to me remains of good?
  To her, perpetual maidenhood,
And unto me no second friend.

VII

Dark house, by which once more I stand
  Here in the long unlovely street,
  Doors, where my heart was used to beat
So quickly, waiting for a hand,

A hand that can be clasped no more –
  Behold me, for I cannot sleep,

And like a guilty thing I creep
At earliest morning to the door.

He is not here; but far away
The noise of life begins again,
And ghastly through the drizzling rain
On the bald street breaks the blank day.

XVIII

Ah yet, ev'n yet, if this might be,
I, falling on his faithful heart,
Would breathing through his lips impart
The life that almost dies in me;

That dies not, but endures with pain,
And slowly forms the firmer mind,
Treasuring the look it cannot find,
The words that are not heard again.

XIX

The Danube to the Severn gave
The darkened heart that beat no more;
They laid him by the pleasant shore,
And in the hearing of the wave.

There twice a day the Severn fills;
The salt sea-water passes by,

And hushes half the babbling Wye,
And makes a silence in the hills.

The Wye is hushed nor moved along,
And hushed my deepest grief of all,
When filled with tears that cannot fall,
I brim with sorrow drowning song.

The tide flows down, the wave again
Is vocal in its wooded walls;
My deeper anguish also falls,
And I can speak a little then.

XX

The lesser griefs that may be said,
That breathe a thousand tender vows,
Are but as servants in a house
Where lies the master newly dead;

Who speak their feeling as it is,
And weep the fullness from the mind:
'It will be hard,' they say, 'to find
Another service such as this.'

My lighter moods are like to these,
That out of words a comfort win;
But there are other griefs within,
And tears that at their fountain freeze;

For by the hearth the children sit,
  Cold in that atmosphere of Death,
  And scarce endure to draw the breath,
Or like to noiseless phantoms flit:

But open converse is there none,
  So much the vital spirits sink
  To see the vacant chair, and think,
'How good! how kind! and he is gone.'

XXI

I sing to him that rests below,
  And, since the grasses round me wave,
  I take the grasses of the grave,
And make them pipes whereon to blow.

The traveller hears me now and then,
  And sometimes harshly will he speak;
  'This fellow would make weakness weak,
And melt the waxen hearts of men.'

Another answers, 'Let him be,
  He loves to make parade of pain,
  That with his piping he may gain
The praise that comes to constancy.'

A third is wroth, 'Is this an hour
  For private sorrow's barren song,

When more and more the people throng
The chairs and thrones of civil power?

'A time to sicken and to swoon,
When Science reaches forth her arms
To feel from world to world, and charms
Her secret from the latest moon?'

Behold, ye speak an idle thing:
Ye never knew the sacred dust:
I do but sing because I must,
And pipe but as the linnets sing:

And one is glad; her note is gay,
For now her little ones have ranged;
And one is sad; her note is changed,
Because her brood is stolen away.

XXIV

And was the day of my delight
As pure and perfect as I say?
The very source and fount of Day
Is dashed with wandering isles of night.

If all was good and fair we met,
This earth had been the Paradise
It never looked to human eyes
Since Adam left his garden yet.

And is it that the haze of grief
Makes former gladness loom so great?
The lowness of the present state,
That sets the past in this relief?

Or that the past will always win
A glory from its being far;
And orb into the perfect star
We saw not, when we moved therein?

XXV

I know that this was Life, – the track
Whereon with equal feet we fared;
And then, as now, the day prepared
The daily burden for the back.

But this it was that made me move
As light as carrier-birds in air;
I loved the weight I had to bear
Because it needed help of Love:

Nor could I weary, heart or limb,
When mighty Love would cleave in twain
The lading of a single pain,
And part it, giving half to him.

XXVII

I envy not in any moods
The captive void of noble rage,
The linnet born within the cage,
That never knew the summer woods:

I envy not the beast that takes
His licence in the field of time,
Unfettered by the sense of crime,
To whom a conscience never wakes;

Nor, what may count itself as blest,
The heart that never plighted troth
But stagnates in the weeds of sloth;
Nor any want-begotten rest.

I hold it true, whate'er befall;
I feel it, when I sorrow most;
'Tis better to have loved and lost
Than never to have loved at all.

XXXI

When Lazarus left his charnel-cave,
And home to Mary's house returned,
Was this demanded – if he yearned
To hear her weeping by his grave?

'Where wert thou, brother, those four days?'
  There lives no record of reply,
  Which telling what it is to die
Had surely added praise to praise.

From every house the neighbours met,
  The streets were filled with joyful sound,
  A solemn gladness even crowned
The purple brows of Olivet.

Behold a man raised up by Christ!
  The rest remaineth unrevealed;
  He told it not; or something sealed
The lips of that Evangelist.

XXXII

Her eyes are homes of silent prayer,
  Nor other thought her mind admits
  But, he was dead, and there he sits,
And he that brought him back is there.

Then one deep love doth supersede
  All other, when her ardent gaze
  Roves from the living brother's face,
And rests upon the Life indeed.

All subtle thought, all curious fears,
  Borne down by gladness so complete,

She bows, she bathes the Saviour's feet
With costly spikenard and with tears.

Thrice blest whose lives are faithful prayers,
Whose loves in higher love endure;
What souls possess themselves so pure,
Or is there blessedness like theirs?

XXXV

Yet if some voice that man could trust
Should murmur from the narrow house,
'The cheeks drop in; the body bows;
Man dies: nor is there hope in dust:'

Might I not say? 'Yet even here,
But for one hour, O Love, I strive
To keep so sweet a thing alive:'
But I should turn mine eyes and hear

The moanings of the homeless sea
The sound of streams that swift or slow
Draw down Aeonian hills, and sow
The dust of continents to be;

And Love would answer with a sigh,
'The sound of that forgetful shore
Will change my sweetness more and more,
Half-dead to know that I shall die.'

O me, what profits it to put
An idle case? If Death were seen
At first as Death, Love had not been,
Or been in narrowest working shut,

Mere fellowship of sluggish moods,
Or in his coarsest Satyr-shape
Had bruised the herb and crushed the grape,
And basked and battened in the woods.

XXXVI

Though truths in manhood darkly join,
Deep-seated in our mystic frame,
We yield all blessing to the name
Of Him that made them current coin;

For Wisdom dealt with mortal powers,
Where truth in closest words shall fail,
When truth embodied in a tale
Shall enter in at lowly doors.

And so the Word had breath, and wrought
With human hands the creed of creeds
In loveliness of perfect deeds,
More strong than all poetic thought;

Which he may read that binds the sheaf,
Or builds the house, or digs the grave,

And those wild eyes that watch the wave
In roarings round the coral reef.

XXXVIII

With weary steps I loiter on,
Though always under altered skies
The purple from the distance dies,
My prospect and horizon gone.

No joy the blowing season gives,
The herald melodies of spring,
But in the songs I love to sing
A doubtful gleam of solace lives.

If any care for what is here
Survive in spirits rendered free,
Then are these songs I sing of thee
Not all ungrateful to thine ear.

XXXIX

Old warder of these buried bones,
And answering now my random stroke
With fruitful cloud and living smoke,
Dark yew, that graspest at the stones

And dippest toward the dreamless head,
To thee too comes the golden hour

When flower is feeling after flower;
But Sorrow – fixt upon the dead,

And darkening the dark graves of men, –
What whispered from her lying lips?
Thy gloom is kindled at the tips,
And passes into gloom again.

L

Be near me when my light is low,
When the blood creeps, and the nerves prick
And tingle; and the heart is sick,
And all the wheels of Being slow.

Be near me when the sensuous frame
Is racked with pangs that conquer trust;
And Time, a maniac scattering dust,
And Life, a Fury slinging flame.

Be near me when my faith is dry,
And men the flies of latter spring,
That lay their eggs, and sting and sing,
And weave their petty cells and die.

Be near me when I fade away,
To point the term of human strife,
And on the low dark verge of life
The twilight of eternal day.

LIV

Oh yet we trust that somehow good
Will be the final goal of ill,
To pangs of nature, sins of will,
Defects of doubt, and taints of blood;

That nothing walks with aimless feet;
That not one life shall be destroyed,
Or cast as rubbish to the void,
When God hath made the pile complete;

That not a worm is cloven in vain;
That not a moth with vain desire
Is shrivelled in a fruitless fire,
Or but subserves another's gain.

Behold, we know not anything;
I can but trust that good shall fall
At last – far off – at last, to all,
And every winter change to spring.

So runs my dream: but what am I?
An infant crying in the night:
An infant crying for the light:
And with no language but a cry.

LV

The wish, that of the living whole
  No life may fail beyond the grave,
  Derives it not from what we have
The likest God within the soul?

Are God and Nature then at strife,
  That Nature lends such evil dreams?
  So careful of the type she seems,
So careless of the single life;

That I, considering everywhere
  Her secret meaning in her deeds,
  And finding that of fifty seeds
She often brings but one to bear,

I falter where I firmly trod,
  And falling with my weight of cares
  Upon the great world's altar-stairs
That slope through darkness up to God,

I stretch lame hands of faith, and grope,
  And gather dust and chaff, and call
  To what I feel is Lord of all,
And faintly trust the larger hope.

LVI

'So careful of the type?' but no.
  From scarpèd cliff and quarried stone
  She cries 'A thousand types are gone:
I care for nothing, all shall go.

'Thou makest thine appeal to me:
  I bring to life, I bring to death:
  The spirit does but mean the breath:
I know no more.' And he, shall he,

Man, her last work, who seemed so fair,
  Such splendid purpose in his eyes,
  Who rolled the psalm to wintry skies,
Who built him fanes of fruitless prayer,

Who trusted God was love indeed
  And love Creation's final law –
  Though Nature, red in tooth and claw
With ravine, shrieked against his creed –

Who loved, who suffered countless ills,
  Who battled for the True, the Just,
  Be blown about the desert dust,
Or sealed within the iron hills?

No more? A monster then, a dream,
  A discord. Dragons of the prime,

That tare each other in their slime,
Were mellow music matched with him.

O life as futile, then, as frail!
O for thy voice to soothe and bless!
What hope of answer, or redress?
Behind the veil, behind the veil.

LVII

Peace; come away: the song of woe
Is after all an earthly song:
Peace; come away: we do him wrong
To sing so wildly: let us go.

Come! let us go: your cheeks are pale;
But half my life I leave behind:
Methinks my friend is richly shrined;
But I shall pass; my work will fail.

Yet in these ears, till hearing dies
One set slow bell will seem to toll
The passing of the sweetest soul
That ever looked with human eyes.

I hear it now, and o'er and o'er,
Eternal greetings to the dead;
And 'Ave, Ave, Ave,' said,
'Adieu, adieu' for evermore.

LVIII

In those sad words I took farewell:
Like echoes in sepulchral halls,
As drop by drop the water falls
In vaults and catacombs, they fell;

And, falling, idly broke the peace
Of hearts that beat from day to day,
Half-conscious of their dying clay,
And those cold crypts where they shall cease.

The high Muse answered: 'Wherefore grieve
Thy brethren with a fruitless tear?
Abide a little longer here,
And thou shalt take a nobler leave.'

LXVII

When on my bed the moonlight falls,
I know that in thy place of rest
By that broad water of the west,
There comes a glory on the walls:

Thy marble bright in dark appears,
As slowly steals a silver flame
Along the letters of thy name,
And o'er the number of thy years.

The mystic glory swims away;
From off my bed the moonlight dies;
And closing eaves of wearied eyes
I sleep till dusk is dipt in grey:

And then I know the mist is drawn
A lucid veil from coast to coast,
And in the dark church like a ghost
Thy tablet glimmers to the dawn.

LXIX

I dreamed there would be Spring no more,
That Nature's ancient power was lost:
The streets were black with smoke and frost,
They chattered trifles at the door:

I wandered from the noisy town,
I found a wood with thorny boughs:
I took the thorns to bind my brows,
I wore them like a civic crown:

I met with scoffs, I met with scorns
From youth and babe and hoary hairs:
They called me in the public squares
The fool that wears a crown of thorns:

They called me fool, they called me child:
I found an angel of the night;

The voice was low, the look was bright;
He looked upon my crown and smiled:

He reached the glory of a hand,
That seemed to touch it into leaf:
The voice was not the voice of grief,
The words were hard to understand.

LXX

I cannot see the features right,
When on the gloom I strive to paint
The face I know; the hues are faint
And mix with hollow masks of night;

Cloud-towers by ghostly masons wrought,
A gulf that ever shuts and gapes,
A hand that points, and pallèd shapes
In shadowy thoroughfares of thought;

And crowds that stream from yawning doors,
And shoals of puckered faces drive;
Dark bulks that tumble half alive,
And lazy lengths on boundless shores;

Till all at once beyond the will
I hear a wizard music roll,
And through a lattice on the soul
Looks thy fair face and makes it still.

LXXVII

What hope is here for modern rhyme
To him, who turns a musing eye
On songs, and deeds, and lives, that lie
Foreshortened in the tract of time?

These mortal lullabies of pain
May bind a book, may line a box,
May serve to curl a maiden's locks;
Or when a thousand moons shall wane

A man upon a stall may find,
And, passing, turn the page that tells
A grief, then changed to something else,
Sung by long-forgotten mind.

But what of that? My darkened ways
Shall ring with music all the same;
To breathe my loss is more than fame,
To utter love more sweet than praise.

LXXXI

Could I have said while he was here,
'My love shall now no further range;
There cannot come a mellower change,
For now is love mature in ear.'

Love, then, had hope of richer store:
  What end is here to my complaint?
  This haunting whisper makes me faint,
'More years had made me love thee more.'

But Death returns an answer sweet:
  'My sudden frost was sudden gain,
  And gave all ripeness to the grain
It might have drawn from after-heat.'

LXXXIII

Dip down upon the northern shore,
  O sweet new-year delaying long;
  Thou doest expectant nature wrong;
Delaying long, delay no more.

What stays thee from the clouded noons,
  Thy sweetness from its proper place?
  Can trouble live with April days,
Or sadness in the summer moons?

Bring orchis, bring the foxglove spire,
  The little speedwell's darling blue,
  Deep tulips dashed with fiery dew,
Laburnums, dropping-wells of fire.

O thou, new-year, delaying long,
  Delayest the sorrow in my blood,

That longs to burst a frozen bud
And flood a fresher throat with song.

LXXXVI

Sweet after showers, ambrosial air,
That rollest from the gorgeous gloom
Of evening over brake and bloom
And meadow, slowly breathing bare

The round of space, and rapt below
Through all the dewy-tasselled wood,
And shadowing down the hornèd flood
In ripples, fan my brows and blow

The fever from my cheek, and sigh
The full new life that feeds thy breath
Throughout my frame, till Doubt and Death,
Ill brethren, let the fancy fly

From belt to belt of crimson seas
On leagues of odour streaming far,
To where in yonder orient star
A hundred spirits whisper 'Peace.'

LXXXVIII

Wild bird, whose warble, liquid sweet,
Rings Eden through the budded quicks,

O tell me where the senses mix,
O tell me where the passions meet,

Whence radiate: fierce extremes employ
Thy spirits in the darkening leaf,
And in the midmost heart of grief
Thy passion clasps a secret joy:

And I – my harp would prelude woe –
I cannot all command the strings;
The glory of the sum of things
Will flash along the chords and go.

XCI

When rosy plumelets tuft the larch,
And rarely pipes the mounted thrush;
Or underneath the barren bush
Flits by the sea-blue bird of March;

Come, wear the form by which I know
Thy spirit in time among thy peers;
The hope of unaccomplished years
Be large and lucid round thy brow.

When summer's hourly-mellowing change
May breathe, with many roses sweet,
Upon the thousand waves of wheat,
That ripple round the lonely grange;

Come: not in watches of the night,
But where the sunbeam broodeth warm,
Come, beauteous in thine after form,
And like a finer light in light.

XCIII

I shall not see thee. Dare I say
No spirit ever brake the band
That stays him from the native land
Where first he walked when claspt in clay?

No visual shade of some one lost,
But he, the Spirit himself, may come
Where all the nerve of sense is numb;
Spirit to Spirit, Ghost to Ghost.

O, therefore from thy sightless range
With gods in unconjectured bliss,
O, from the distance of the abyss
Of tenfold-complicated change,

Descend, and touch, and enter; hear
The wish too strong for words to name;
That in this blindness of the frame
My Ghost may feel that thine is near.

XCIV

How pure at heart and sound in head,
With what divine affections bold
Should be the man whose thought would hold
An hour's communion with the dead.

In vain shalt thou, or any, call
The spirits from their golden day,
Except, like them, thou too canst say,
My spirit is at peace with all.

They haunt the silence of the breast,
Imaginations calm and fair,
The memory like a cloudless air,
The conscience as a sea at rest:

But when the heart is full of din,
And doubt beside the portal waits,
They can but listen at the gates,
And hear the household jar within.

XCV

By night we lingered on the lawn,
For underfoot the herb was dry;
And genial warmth; and o'er the sky
The silvery haze of summer drawn;

And calm that let the tapers burn
  Unwavering: not a cricket chirred:
  The brook alone far-off was heard,
And on the board the fluttering urn:

And bats went round in fragrant skies,
  And wheeled or lit the filmy shapes
  That haunt the dusk, with ermine capes
And woolly breasts and beaded eyes;

While now we sang old songs that pealed
  From knoll to knoll, where, couched at ease,
  The white kine glimmered, and the trees
Laid their dark arms about the field.

But when those others, one by one,
  Withdrew themselves from me and night,
  And in the house light after light
Went out, and I was all alone,

A hunger seized my heart; I read
  Of that glad year which once had been,
  In those fallen leaves which kept their green,
The noble letters of the dead:

And strangely on the silence broke
  The silent-speaking words, and strange

Was love's dumb cry defying change
To test his worth; and strangely spoke

The faith, the vigour, bold to dwell
On doubts that drive the coward back,
And keen through wordy snares to track
Suggestion to her inmost cell.

So word by word, and line by line,
The dead man touched me from the past,
And all at once it seemed at last
His living soul was flashed on mine,

And mine in his was wound, and whirled
About empyreal heights of thought,
And came on that which is, and caught
The deep pulsations of the world,

Aeonian music measuring out
The steps of Time – the shocks of Chance –
The blows of Death. At length my trance
Was cancelled, stricken through with doubt.

Vague words! but ah, how hard to frame
In matter-moulded forms of speech,
Or ev'n for intellect to reach
Through memory that which I became:

Till now the doubtful dusk revealed
The knolls once more where, couched at ease,
The white kine glimmered, and the trees
Laid their dark arms about the field:

And sucked from out the distant gloom
A breeze began to tremble o'er
The large leaves of the sycamore,
And fluctuate all the still perfume,

And gathering freshlier overhead,
Rocked the full-foliaged elms, and swung
The heavy-folded rose, and flung
The lilies to and fro, and said

'The dawn, the dawn,' and died away;
And East and West, without a breath,
Mixt their dim lights, like life and death,
To broaden into boundless day.

CIV

The time draws near the birth of Christ;
The moon is hid, the night is still;
A single church below the hill
Is pealing, folded in the mist.

A single peal of bells below,
That wakens at this hour of rest

A single murmur in the breast,
That these are not the bells I know.

Like strangers' voices here they sound,
In lands where not a memory strays
Nor landmark breathes of other days,
But all is new unhallowed ground.

CVI

Ring out, wild bells, to the wild sky,
The flying cloud, the frosty light:
The year is dying in the night;
Ring out, wild bells, and let him die.

Ring out the old, ring in the new,
Ring, happy bells, across the snow:
The year is going, let him go;
Ring out the false, ring in the true.

Ring out the grief that saps the mind,
For those that here we see no more;
Ring out the feud of rich and poor,
Ring in redress to all mankind.

Ring out a slowly dying cause,
And ancient forms of party strife;
Ring in the nobler modes of life,
With sweeter manners, purer laws.

Ring out the want, the care, the sin,
The faithless coldness of the times;
Ring out, ring out my mournful rhymes
But ring the fuller minstrel in.

Ring out false pride in place and blood,
The civic slander and the spite;
Ring in the love of truth and right,
Ring in the common love of good.

Ring out old shapes of foul disease;
Ring out the narrowing lust of gold;
Ring out the thousand wars of old,
Ring in the thousand years of peace.

Ring in the valiant man and free,
The larger heart, the kindlier hand;
Ring out the darkness of the land,
Ring in the Christ that is to be.

CXV

Now fades the last long streak of snow,
Now burgeons every maze of quick
About the flowering squares, and thick
By ashen roots the violets blow.

Now rings the woodland loud and long,
The distance takes a lovelier hue,

And drowned in yonder living blue
The lark becomes a sightless song.

Now dance the lights on lawn and lea,
The flocks are whiter down the vale,
And milkier every milky sail
On winding stream or distant sea;

Where now the seamew pipes, or dives
In yonder greening gleam, and fly
The happy birds, that change their sky
To build and brood; that live their lives

From land to land; and in my breast
Spring wakens too; and my regret
Becomes an April violet,
And buds and blossoms like the rest.

CXVI

Is it, then, regret for buried time
That keenlier in sweet April wakes,
And meets the year, and gives and takes
The colours of the crescent prime?

Not all: the songs, the stirring air,
The life re-orient out of dust,
Cry through the sense to hearten trust
In that which made the world so fair.

Not all regret: the face will shine
  Upon me, while I muse alone;
  And that dear voice, I once have known,
Still speak to me of me and mine:

Yet less of sorrow lives in me
  For days of happy commune dead;
  Less yearning for the friendship fled,
Than some strong bond which is to be.

CXVII

O days and hours, your work is this,
  To hold me from my proper place,
  A little while from his embrace,
For fuller gain of after bliss:

That out of distance might ensue
  Desire of nearness doubly sweet;
  And unto meeting when we meet,
Delight a hundredfold accrue,

For every grain of sand that runs,
  And every span of shade that steals,
  And every kiss of toothèd wheels,
And all the courses of the suns.

CXIX

Doors, where my heart was used to beat
So quickly, not as one that weeps
I come once more; the city sleeps;
I smell the meadow in the street;

I hear a chirp of birds; I see
Betwixt the black fronts long-withdrawn
A light-blue lane of early dawn,
And think of early days and thee,

And bless thee, for thy lips are bland
And bright the friendship of thine eye;
And in my thoughts with scarce a sigh
I take the pressure of thine hand.

CXXIII

There rolls the deep where grew the tree.
O earth, what changes hast thou seen!
There where the long street roars, hath been
The stillness of the central sea.

The hills are shadows, and they flow
From form to form, and nothing stands;
They melt like mist, the solid lands,
Like clouds they shape themselves and go.

But in my spirit will I dwell,
And dream my dream, and hold it true;
For though my lips may breathe adieu,
I cannot think the thing farewell.

CXXVI

Love is and was my Lord and King,
And in his presence I attend
To hear the tidings of my friend,
Which every hour his couriers bring.

Love is and was my King and Lord,
And will be, though as yet I keep
Within his court on earth, and sleep
Encompassed by his faithful guard,

And hear at times a sentinel
Who moves about from place to place,
And whispers to the worlds of space,
In the deep night, that all is well.

CXXIX

Dear friend, far off, my lost desire,
So far, so near in woe and weal;
O loved the most, when most I feel
There is a lower and a higher;

Known and unknown; human, divine;
  Sweet human hand and lips and eye;
  Dear heavenly friend that canst not die,
Mine, mine, for ever, ever mine;

Strange friend, past, present, and to be;
  Loved deeplier, darklier understood;
  Behold, I dream a dream of good,
And mingle all the world with thee.

CXXX

Thy voice is on the rolling air;
  I hear thee where the waters run;
  Thou standest in the rising sun,
And in the setting thou art fair.

What art thou then? I cannot guess;
  But though I seem in star and flower
  To feel thee some diffusive power,
I do not therefore love thee less:

My love involves the love before;
  My love is vaster passion now;
  Though mixed with God and Nature thou,
I seem to love thee more and more.

Far off thou art, but ever nigh;
I have thee still, and I rejoice;
I prosper, circled with thy voice;
I shall not lose thee though I die.

CXXXI

O living will that shalt endure
When all that seems shall suffer shock,
Rise in the spiritual rock,
Flow through our deeds and make them pure,

That we may lift from out of dust
A voice as unto him that hears,
A cry above the conquered years
To one that with us works, and trust,

With faith that comes of self-control,
The truths that never can be proved
Until we close with all we loved,
And all we flow from, soul in soul.

[EPILOGUE]

O true and tried, so well and long,
Demand not thou a marriage lay;
In that it is thy marriage day
Is music more than any song.

Nor have I felt so much of bliss
  Since first he told me that he loved
  A daughter of our house; nor proved
Since that dark day a day like this;

Though I since then have numbered o'er
  Some thrice three years: they went and came,
  Remade the blood and changed the frame,
And yet is love not less, but more;

No longer caring to embalm
  In dying songs a dead regret,
  But like a statue solid-set,
And moulded in colossal calm.

Regret is dead, but love is more
  Than in the summers that are flown,
  For I myself with these have grown
To something greater than before;

Which makes appear the songs I made
  As echoes out of weaker times,
  As half but idle brawling rhymes,
The sport of random sun and shade.

But where is she, the bridal flower,
  That must be made a wife ere noon?

She enters, glowing like the moon
Of Eden on its bridal bower:

On me she bends her blissful eyes
And then on thee; they meet thy look
And brighten like the star that shook
Betwixt the palms of paradise.

O when her life was yet in bud,
He too foretold the perfect rose.
For thee she grew, for thee she grows
For ever, and as fair as good.

And thou art worthy; full of power;
As gentle; liberal-minded, great,
Consistent; wearing all that weight
Of learning lightly like a flower.

But now set out: the noon is near,
And I must give away the bride;
She fears not, or with thee beside
And me behind her, will not fear.

For I that danced her on my knee,
That watched her on her nurse's arm,
That shielded all her life from harm
At last must part with her to thee;

Now waiting to be made a wife,
  Her feet, my darling, on the dead;
  Their pensive tablets round her head,
And the most living words of life

Breathed in her ear. The ring is on,
  The 'wilt thou' answered, and again
  The 'wilt thou' asked, till out of twain
Her sweet 'I will' has made you one.

Now sign your names, which shall be read,
  Mute symbols of a joyful morn,
  By village eyes as yet unborn;
The names are signed, and overhead

Begins the clash and clang that tells
  The joy to every wandering breeze;
  The blind wall rocks, and on the trees
The dead leaf trembles to the bells.

O happy hour, and happier hours
  Await them. Many a merry face
  Salutes them – maidens of the place,
That pelt us in the porch with flowers.

O happy hour, behold the bride
  With him to whom her hand I gave.

They leave the porch, they pass the grave
That has today its sunny side.

Today the grave is bright for me,
For them the light of life increased,
Who stay to share the morning feast,
Who rest tonight beside the sea.

Let all my genial spirits advance
To meet and greet a whiter sun;
My drooping memory will not shun
The foaming grape of eastern France.

It circles round, and fancy plays,
And hearts are warmed and faces bloom,
As drinking health to bride and groom
We wish them store of happy days.

Nor count me all to blame if I
Conjecture of a stiller guest,
Perchance, perchance, among the rest,
And, though in silence, wishing joy.

But they must go, the time draws on,
And those white-favoured horses wait;
They rise, but linger; it is late;
Farewell, we kiss, and they are gone.

A shade falls on us like the dark
  From little cloudlets on the grass,
  But sweeps away as out we pass
To range the woods, to roam the park,

Discussing how their courtship grew,
  And talk of others that are wed,
  And how she looked, and what he said,
And back we come at fall of dew.

Again the feast, the speech, the glee,
  The shade of passing thought, the wealth
  Of words and wit, the double health,
The crowning cup, the three-times-three,

And last the dance; – till I retire:
  Dumb is that tower which spake so loud,
  And high in heaven the streaming cloud,
And on the downs a rising fire:

And rise, O moon, from yonder down,
  Till over down and over dale
  All night the shining vapour sail
And pass the silent-lighted town,

The white-faced halls, the glancing rills,
  And catch at every mountain head,

And o'er the friths that branch and spread
Their sleeping silver through the hills;

And touch with shade the bridal doors,
With tender gloom the roof, the wall;
And breaking let the splendour fall
To spangle all the happy shores

By which they rest, and ocean sounds,
And, star and system rolling past,
A soul shall draw from out the vast
And strike his being into bounds,

And, moved through life of lower phase,
Result in man, be born and think,
And act and love, a closer link
Betwixt us and the crowning race

Of those that, eye to eye, shall look
On knowledge; under whose command
Is Earth and Earth's, and in their hand
Is Nature like an open book;

No longer half-akin to brute,
For all we thought and loved and did,
And hoped, and suffered, is but seed
Of what in them is flower and fruit;

Whereof the man, that with me trod
  This planet, was a noble type
  Appearing ere the times were ripe,
That friend of mine who lives in God,

That God, which ever lives and loves,
  One God, one law, one element,
  And one far-off divine event,
To which the whole creation moves.

CROSSING THE BAR

Sunset and evening star,
    And one clear call for me!
And may there be no moaning of the bar,
    When I put out to sea,

But such a tide as moving seems asleep,
    Too full for sound and foam,
When that which drew from out the boundless deep
    Turns again home.

Twilight and evening bell,
    And after that the dark!
And may there be no sadness of farewell,
    When I embark;

For though from out our bourne of Time and Place
    The flood may bear me far,
I hope to see my Pilot face to face
    When I have crost the bar.